BRINGING OUTDOOR SCIENCE IN

Thrifty Classroom Lessons

MW00630435

BRINGING OUTDOOR SCIENCE IN

Thrifty Classroom Lessons

— STEVE RICH —

press

National Science Teachers Association

Arlington, Virginia

Claire Reinburg, Director
Jennifer Horak, Managing Editor
Andrew Cooke, Senior Editor
Wendy Rubin, Associate Editor
Agnes Bannigan, Associate Editor
Amy America, Book Acquisitions
  Coordinator

ART AND DESIGN
Will Thomas Jr., Director
Joe Butera, Senior Graphic Designer, cover
  and interior design
Cover photos by Vladimir Semenov,
  Guillermo Lobo, MBPHOTO, INC.,
  stock-graphy, ooyoo for iStock

PRINTING AND PRODUCTION
Catherine Lorrain, Director

SCILINKS
Tyson Brown, Director
Virginie L. Chokouanga, Customer Service
  and Database Coordinator

NATIONAL SCIENCE TEACHERS ASSOCIATION
Francis Q. Eberle, PhD, Executive Director
David Beacom, Publisher
1840 Wilson Blvd., Arlington, VA 22201
www.nsta.org/store
For customer service inquiries, please call 800-277-5300.

Copyright © 2012 by the National Science Teachers Association.
All rights reserved. Printed in the United States of America.
15 14 13 12   4 3 2 1

NSTA is committed to publishing material that promotes the best in inquiry-based science education. However, conditions of actual use may vary, and the safety procedures and practices described in this book are intended to serve only as a guide. Additional precautionary measures may be required. NSTA and the authors do not warrant or represent that the procedures and practices in this book meet any safety code or standard of federal, state, or local regulations. NSTA and the authors disclaim any liability for personal injury or damage to property arising out of or relating to the use of this book, including any of the recommendations, instructions, or materials contained therein.

PERMISSIONS
Book purchasers may photocopy, print, or e-mail up to five copies of an NSTA book chapter for personal use only; this does not include display or promotional use. Elementary, middle, and high school teachers may reproduce forms, sample documents, and single NSTA book chapters needed for classroom or noncommercial, professional-development use only. E-book buyers may download files to multiple personal devices but are prohibited from posting the files to third-party servers or websites, or from passing files to non-buyers. For additional permission to photocopy or use material electronically from this NSTA Press book, please contact the Copyright Clearance Center (CCC) (*www.copyright.com*; 978-750-8400). Please access *www.nsta.org/permissions* for further information about NSTA's rights and permissions policies.

 Featuring SciLinks®—a new way of connecting text and the internet. Up-to-the minute online content, classroom ideas, and other materials are just a click away. For more information, go to www.scilinks.org/Faq.aspx.

eISBN 978-1-936959-87-7

Library of Congress Cataloging-in-Publication Data
Rich, Steve, 1962-
  Bringing outdoor science in : thrifty classroom lessons / by Steve Rich.
    p. cm.
  Includes bibliographical references and index.
  ISBN 978-1-936959-04-4
  1. Science--Study and teaching (Elementary)--Activity programs. 2. Natural history--Study and teaching (Elementary)--Activity programs. 3. Outdoor education. I. Title.
  QH53.R48 2012
  508.071--dc23
                    2011047208

FSC
www.fsc.org
MIX
Paper from
responsible sources
FSC® C011935

CONTENTS

— 1 —
Greening the School

Page 1

— 2 —
Insects

Page 29

— 3 —
Plants

Page 57

— 4 —
Rocks and Soils

Page 77

— 5 —
Water

Page 101

— 6 —
In the Sky

Page 121

DEDICATION

This book is dedicated with love, deep respect, and admiration, to my mother, June Coleman Rich, who understood my need as a child to bring outdoor creatures inside, and instinctively knew more than me that one day all the lizards, snakes, frogs, and turtles would propel me toward trying to making a difference for young people and their teachers.

"A mother's heart is a child's school room." ~ Henry Ward Beecher

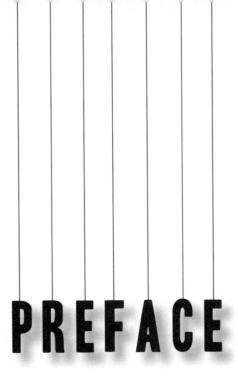

PREFACE

During more than a dozen years of planning, building, using, and writing about outdoor classrooms, I have met many, many teachers who have discovered the joy of taking students out to the school yard for engaging lessons and learning. At the same time, I have met a number of teachers who have told me they are never going outside with their students. While it's almost foreign to me to consider remaining in my classroom when there is so much science in the school yard, I understand that in some situations this is discouraged by administrators or complicated by a host of factors beyond the control of the teacher. So as a result of my conversations with these teachers, I decided to write *Bringing Outdoor Science In: Thrifty Classroom Lessons.*

In this follow-up to *Outdoor Science: A Practical Guide,* you'll find many units and lessons that can be taught indoors or outdoors. Students participating in these lessons will sometimes use natural materials. One of the best parts of this type of lesson is that the materials from outdoors are free! If you are teaching a lesson using a leaf or a rock, you can simply step outside and gather the materials. There's no need to pull out your science catalog and create a purchase order. Who has time for that anyway?

This book may be used as is for upper elementary and middle grades. Possible adaptations for primary grades are noted in the section "Grade-Level Considerations" within each lesson. In this book the various grade levels are defined as follows: *primary* refers to grades K through 2, *upper elementary* refers to grades 3 through 5, and *middle* refers to grades 6 through 8.

It is my hope that as you use these lessons, you will see the value in taking your class outdoors. The experience of learning outdoors enriches the environmental knowledge base for young people, giving them the insight to become better stewards of natural resources throughout their lives. If you decide not to take students outdoors, certainly you will encourage them to explore just by bringing some of the outdoors into your own classroom.

ACKNOWLEDGMENTS

As *Bringing Outdoor Science In* continues my journey through the world of science education, it is important to acknowledge those who have traveled along this road with me. Sometimes these fellow travelers find feathers for my artifact boxes, provide caterpillar care at the "science lab" (dining room table), or at least pretend to be excited when I make the best-seller list. The primary fellow travelers in the order they hopped on the *Outdoor Science* school bus are June Coleman Rich, Cathy Rich Robinson, Spencer Anthony Rich, and Glenn Russell Bilanin.

The professional fellow travelers are too numerous to name individually, but they include members of the professional organizations that give me such inspiration and joy—National Science Teachers Association (NSTA), Georgia Science Teachers Association (GSTA), Georgia Science Supervisors Association (GSSA), Georgia Youth Science & Technology Center (GYSTC), Council of State Science Supervisors (CSSS), Council for Elementary Science International (CESI), and particularly the Society of Elementary Presidential Awardees (SEPA). My life is so enriched by the people I see at meetings and conferences throughout the country—including the NSTA Press staff members who make being an author such a joy.

My students have been a particular source of inspiration to me, and many of the lessons in this book were born in the classrooms at my schools in Georgia. I cannot thank all of my students individually, so I will choose one to represent them all. Shadra Tomei was a student in my sixth-grade science class years ago and is now a fourth-grade teacher who often allows me the honor of co-teaching science in her classroom, trying out new lesson ideas with her students. I am so proud of Shadra, as I am of every student who ever tried his or her best in class, and goes on in life to be a hardworking citizen and hopefully a steward of the environment as a result of experiences in my outdoor classrooms.

I will also thank the traveler whom I carry only in my heart, my late father, Rochell Rich Jr., who worked so hard to make it possible for my childhood to be enriched with endless outdoor adventures on the water, in the woods, at campgrounds, on farms, and on barrier islands. He still guides me through uncharted waters and on new paths through the woods.

ABOUT THE AUTHOR

As a science teacher in elementary and middle schools, Steve Rich created two outdoor classrooms that were honored with NSTA awards—the Ciba Exemplary Science Teaching Award and the Ohaus Award for Innovations in Science Teaching. His professional experience includes writing books for students and teachers and serving as a science specialist for the Georgia Department of Education and as the coordinator of the Youth Science & Technology Center at the University of West Georgia. He is a frequent NSTA presenter and author of the NSTA Press best seller *Outdoor Science: A Practical Guide.*

Steve is a National Board Certified teacher and a recipient of the Presidential Award for Excellence in Science Teaching. He was a district director of NSTA and president of the Georgia Science Teachers Association. He is a graduate of the University of Georgia and Georgia State University. More information about the author is available at *www.sarinkbooks.com.*

Correlation to National Science Education Standards

	Content Standards		Lessons
Physical Science	K–4	Properties of objects and materials	pp. 80, 84, 92, 110
	5–8	Properties and changes of properties in matter	pp. 80, 84, 92, 110
	K–4	Position and motion of objects	pp. 94, 96, 98, 132
	5–8	Motions and forces	pp. 94, 96, 98, 108, 132
	K–4	Light, heat, and magnetism	p. 126
	5–8	Transfer of energy	pp. 8, 38, 62, 108, 138
Life Science	K–4	Characteristics of organisms	pp. 32, 36, 42, 44, 54, 64, 66, 74, 134
	5–8	Structure and function in living systems	pp. 42, 44, 46, 48, 50, 52, 54, 60, 62, 64, 66, 68, 70, 72, 74, 118, 134
	K–4	Life cycles of organisms	p. 50
	5–8	Reproduction and heredity	pp. 42, 44, 50, 66
	K–4	Organisms and environments	pp. 36, 48, 52, 62, 112, 134
	5–8	Regulation and behavior	pp. 32, 36, 60
	5–8	Populations and ecosystems	pp. 38, 40, 46, 48, 52, 70, 72, 112, 134
	5–8	Diversity and adaptations of organisms	pp. 42, 44, 50, 52, 54, 60, 62, 64, 66, 68, 70, 112, 134
Earth and Space Science	K–4	Properties of Earth materials	pp. 80, 84, 86, 90, 92, 94, 110
	5–8	Structure of the Earth system	pp. 80, 84, 86, 88, 90, 92, 94, 96, 98, 104, 106, 108, 110, 112, 114, 116, 118, 124, 126, 130, 132, 138
	K–4	Objects in the sky	pp. 124, 126, 130, 132, 134, 136, 138
	5–8	Earth's history	pp. 80, 84, 86, 88, 130
	K–4	Changes in Earth and sky	pp. 94, 96, 98, 116, 136
	5–8	Earth in the solar system	pp. 126, 130, 132
Science and Technology	K–4	Abilities to distinguish natural objects/manmade	pp. 64, 66, 80, 84, 86, 90, 92
	K–4/5–8	Abilities of technological design	pp. 12, 74, 88, 106, 138
	K–4/5–8	Understanding about science and technology	pp. 12, 88, 106, 138
Science in Personal and Social Perspectives	K–4/5–8	Personal health	
	K–4	Characteristics and changes in populations	p. 38
	5–8	Populations, resources, and environments	pp. 38, 40, 70, 72
	K–4	Types of resources	pp. 4, 8, 72, 108, 138
	5–8	Natural hazard	p. 116
	K–4	Changes in environments	pp. 94, 96, 98, 116
	5–8	Risks and benefits	pp. 116, 136
	K–4/5–8	Science and technology in local challenges/society	pp. 12, 74, 88, 106, 108, 138
History and Nature of Science	K–4/5–8	Science as a human endeavor	pp. 12, 26, 74, 88, 106, 108, 138
	5–8	Nature of science	
	5–8	History of science	pp. 74, 88

SAFETY NOTES

Every school or school system should have a science safety plan, which may include student safety contracts or a uniform set of lab rules. In addition to what your school system requires, here are some common-sense safety considerations specifically addressing the lessons and ideas in this book:

1. Provide students with a lab safety form or science activity safety form that outlines general science safety procedures. You can use your school system's standard form, if available. If you teach in an elementary school that does not use a standard form, check with a middle school science teacher. The safety form should be sent home to be signed by parents.

2. Students should thoroughly wash their hands after any visits to the school yard and after handling any materials that have been taken in from outdoors.

3. Review students' records for allergies such as those to specific plants or stinging insects.

4. Protective equipment, including but not limited to vinyl gloves, aprons, and eye goggles, is encouraged for the activities in this book.

5. Use care when students are asked to use sharp objects (such as those in dissection kits, toothpicks, pipe cleaners, straight pins, rocks, or arrowheads).

6. When gathering any objects outdoors (rocks, soil, insects, etc.), it is best to look for locations that have not been sprayed with pesticides, herbicides, or other chemicals.

7. When working with water indoors, completely clean up any spills.

8. When working outdoors, students should be reminded not to look directly into the Sun.

GREENING THE SCHOOL

Teaching about the natural, outdoor environment indoors can be done well, but it can be even more effective if the indoor environment is nature-friendly or "green" (to use the current lingo). Just trying to teach the value of a tree, for instance, seems a little more difficult if done in an atmosphere of paper waste. The same goes for teaching about taking care of creeks, streams, and rivers. If water is being wasted indoors, how can we effectively teach respect and stewardship of water sources outdoors?

The lessons in this chapter may be used at the beginning of the school year to establish a culture of "going green" for the entire school year. Another logical time of year to consider a unit of these lessons would be the period surrounding Earth Day. Although these lessons do not constitute an entire unit, together they can help you launch an Earth Day unit or school recycling/greening program. If you would rather choose individual lessons from this chapter, you can choose lessons that are relevant to other topics in your classroom. For example, the "Saving Water" lesson might fit in well with a study of the water cycle. If you also teach mathematics, consider using some of the lessons that include gathering data to support math instruction. The lessons related to recycling include addition, multiplication, and estimation. These lessons would be

good choices for putting concrete examples into the mathematics lessons of your students.

Technology is constantly providing new ways to reduce the use of paper, and it also gives us tools to track the progress of efforts to go green. For example, if your school has handheld data devices with temperature probes, your students could use the probes to track the temperature inside a compost container. Instructional options for going green will likely increase between the time this is written and the time you read it, thus giving you even more reason to encourage your students to "green" their daily practices at home and at school.

If some of these lessons prove to be impractical in the regular classroom, consider using them with a science club or any other group of students after school. Regardless of the setting, lessons on improving the recycling and energy-saving efforts of your students and fellow teachers can have a positive effect on your school and even on your community.

Resources

Websites

- *www.captainplanetfoundation.org*
- *www.kidsbegreen.org*
- *www.meetthegreens.org*
- *www.naaee.net*
- *www.pltgreenschools.org*

Children's Literature

- *Compost Stew: An A to Z Recipe for the Earth* by Mary McKenna Siddals (Tricycle Press, 2010)
- *Earth Day Hooray* by Stuart Murphy (HarperCollins, 2004)
- *Girls Gone Green* by Lynn Hirshfield (Puffin, 2010)

DON'T FORGET!

- Students should thoroughly wash their hands after any visits to the school yard and after handling any materials that have been taken in from outdoors.

- Review students' records for allergies such as those to specific plants or stinging insects.

- When gathering any objects outdoors (rocks, soil, insects, etc.), it is best to look for locations that have not been sprayed with pesticides, herbicides, or other chemicals.

For a full list of safety tips, see page xi.

Objectives

Students will gather data to support the need for a possible school recycling program. Students will estimate the number of trees needed to produce the paper used in one school year at this particular school.

Topic: Recycling
Go to: www.scilinks.org
Code: BOS001

Why/How to Use This Lesson

Students need to understand that trees are the origin of paper and to discover ways to reduce the consumption of natural resources. Some paper industry experts estimate that it takes 6% of one tree to make one ream (500 sheets) of copy paper (nonrecycled). Another often-cited statistic is that it takes 17 trees to make one ton of paper. Some interesting statistics about making paper are found in "How Much Paper Can Be Made From a Tree?" at *www.tappi.org/paperu/ all_about_paper/earth_answers/earthanswers_ howmuch.pdf.*

Materials

calculator, recycling bins (optional), student worksheet

Procedures and Tips

1. Have a discussion with students about the origin of paper being trees, and share some information with them about the quantity of trees needed to make paper. You may include other related information (e.g., the process by which paper is made) or ask students to do some research on the topic.

2. Ask each student to keep track of the amount of paper he or she uses in one day for school (including homework). For purposes of this activity, consider standard paper that is usually measured as 8 ½ x 11 in., or notebook paper. If students use index cards, sticky notes, or other small pieces of paper, these may be recorded in fractions or decimals (or several may be added together to equal one piece of paper).

3. Students should record information on the worksheet provided and work with a small group of other students to compile data.

4. Consider asking other teachers in your grade level to do the same activity with their students.

Grade-Level Considerations

For primary grades, consider making this a class project rather than an individual assignment. Keep track of the paper usage on chart paper or a graph on a whiteboard or dry erase board.

Assessment/Next Steps

Review student data for reasonable figures. Hold a class discussion for some qualitative data on the numbers that were gathered. If possible, involve the entire school in gathering data. If not, students can make predictions based on the evidence gathered in your classroom. After conducting this exercise, students may work as a team to establish an actual recycling program in the school. Consider inviting members from a community recycling program, such as local government or private garbage collection services.

Sample Discussion Questions

- Is the amount of paper you used today more or less than what you expected? Why or why not?

- Is the amount of paper used today different for any obvious reason? Explain. (Example: "A classmate forgot his paper and I loaned him 15 pieces.")

RECYCLING SCHOOL PAPER

Name: _____ Date: _____

Think about how much paper you use for your assignments in one day at school. Don't forget paper used for homework. Make a small mark in the box below for every piece of paper you use during <u>one day</u>.

Count all of the marks. How many pieces of paper did you use? _____

Get together with three other students in your class after you have added up your total for the day. Add the totals from all four of you together. How many pieces did the four of you use? What was the average? _____

How can you determine the daily total for your entire class and the daily average of one person in your class?

_____

_____

Keep a record of the paper you use for school during one week in the chart below.

	Monday	Tuesday	Wednesday	Thursday	Friday	Weekly Total
Number of Pieces of Paper						

How could you reduce the number of pieces of paper that you use personally each day? Think of at least three ways.

_____

_____

How could you figure out the average number of pieces of paper used per day by a typical student in your school? _____

_____

_____

After estimating how much paper is used in your school, try to translate this into the number of trees it takes to provide paper for your school. You may need additional information, such as how many days are in a school year, which can usually be found on a school system calendar. With adult supervision, you can use the internet to get reliable data on the amount of paper that can come from an average tree.

_____

_____

_____

Objective

Students will recognize the ability to conserve natural resources through using less paper, with the goal of going totally paperless in the classroom.

Topic: Conservation
Go to: www.scilinks.org
Code: BOS002

Why/How to Use This Lesson

This lesson is best used following the previous lesson, "Recycling School Paper." It is the next step, and together these two lessons can be used to help launch a schoolwide paper recycling program and to generally reduce paper consumption.

Materials

electronic means to deliver the class worksheet

Procedures and Tips

1. If possible, find a way to deliver this lesson in a paperless manner. Instead of handing out printed worksheets, consider sending them to students via e-mail or posting on a school or classroom website.

2. Project the class worksheet in the classroom. Using a smart board, dry erase board, or overhead projector, record answers and data on the class worksheet.

3. Facilitate discussion regarding the possibility of and practical measures for going paperless for a day.

4. Make the necessary arrangements to plan a paperless day (to the extent possible) in your classroom, grade level, or school.

Grade-Level Considerations

If the "Recycling School Paper" lesson was done as a class project with primary grades, do the same with this lesson to make it appropriate for younger students. Focus on reusing classroom materials and use an overhead projector rather than paper. Discuss why you would reuse materials and why a projector would be preferable to using paper. Younger students should ask teachers just the first question of the survey (willingness to have one paperless day); these students should work in pairs so they are more comfortable talking to teachers.

Assessment/Next Steps

Assess student understanding from participation in the classroom discussion. If the paperless day is done on a limited basis (just your class or grade level), make school administrators aware of it and attempt to have a schoolwide paperless day. A paperless day could serve as a launch event for a paper recycling program.

Sample Discussion Questions

- Describe some of the ways you were able to work around using paper.

- How were electronics and technology helpful in avoiding the use of paper?

GOING PAPERLESS

Name: _____ Date: _____

What are some electronic tools that can be used to help a class have a paperless lesson?

Do not write these on paper. Use a word processing program on a computer or an erasable marker, or simply answer in a class discussion. Your teacher will try to provide a paperless method to answer.
If on a whiteboard or other electronic means, put answers here:

_____

_____

_____

_____

Take a survey of other teachers in your school with these two simple questions:

1. As a teacher, would you consider having a paperless assignment at least one day per week?

2. If teaching a paperless lesson, what technology would help you? (examples include cell phone, computer, and projector)

(Try to convince the teachers you interview to e-mail their answers to the teacher giving you this assignment.)

Responses to Question 1	Yes	No
Number of Teachers		

Responses to question 2 (electronic resources teachers would use to deliver lessons):

_____

_____

_____

Discuss a plan for going paperless for a day. This could be in your classroom or as a grade-level or whole-school project. What would be the barriers?

Objectives

Students will be able to distinguish organic material from nonorganic material and determine which materials should be composted. Students will be able to observe and describe the process of decomposition of plant material.

Topic: Composting
Go to: www.scilinks.org
Code: BOS003

Why/How to Use This Lesson

In the process of "greening" the school, it may seem obvious to recycle paper, bottles, cans, and any materials for which there are widespread recycling programs available to the public. It may not be as easy to recycle cafeteria waste, but it is certainly well worth the effort as a means to teach students about decomposition of living things—plants in particular. Establishing a small compost bin in your classroom is easy and sets up many opportunities for exploration.

Materials

Compost Stew (see the "Resources" section at the beginning of this chapter); plastic container with top that seals; cafeteria scraps such as fruit peelings, apple cores, lettuce scraps, or any other uncooked plant material; earthworms or mealworms; six plastic shoe boxes (optional); scales (optional); graphing calculators with temperature probes (optional); student worksheet

Procedures and Tips

1. Before starting this lesson, let the school cafeteria manager know that you would like to collect simple waste such as apple cores, banana peels, orange peels, and salad bar scraps. The manager may be able to provide an appropriate container, such as a large plastic pickle bucket with a resealable top, for transporting materials from the cafeteria.

(SAFETY NOTE: Check student records for food allergies.)

2. Have a class discussion about composting. Ask if any students have a compost bin at home. Read aloud the book *Compost Stew* and ask students for their thoughts. Ask how your class could produce its own compost.

3. Provide a compost container for the classroom. Depending on space and materials available, you can have one large compost container or several smaller ones. If using smaller ones, consider using about six plastic shoe boxes; this would make it possible to give each cooperative group in the class their own bin to observe over time.

4. Work out a collection system for students to retrieve material from the cafeteria to put in their bin(s). You may want to have them collect material for a week in a large bucket and then put the material into smaller bins at the end of the week. This may yield a better variety of organic material.

5. Living earthworms or mealworms aid in the compost process. You may obtain these from a reputable science vendor, a pet shop, or a bait store. Students should put about three or four earthworms or mealworms in each container.

6. Either assign specific data gathering to each group or facilitate their decision on what data they will gather.

Grade-Level Considerations

For primary grades, start the compost bin after reading the book but just focus on one large bin in your classroom rather than several smaller bins for groups. Rather than assign groups to gather data, one aspect of gathering data can be decided on by the teacher with a question such as "How many pieces of food are easily identified in the compost?"

Assessment/Next Steps

This lesson lends itself to continuing and expanding beyond your classroom, but the single-classroom component is important to help students make close observations and understand the process. After completing the classroom part of the lesson, consider working with the cafeteria manager and school administrator on a plan to involve additional teachers and students. If possible, set up an outdoor compost bin to accommodate a greater amount of compostable material.

Sample Discussion Questions

- Why would it be helpful to compost cafeteria waste?

- How do different materials respond to being in the compost bin? How can you describe the decomposition process?

COMPOSTING CAFETERIA WASTE

Name: _____ Date: _____

What is the purpose of a compost bin? What are the benefits?

_____

_____

Describe the compost bin you will observe. What type of container will you use? What specific items will you put in it?

_____

_____

_____

Use words and numbers to record what you are putting into the compost. If possible, weigh the contents (for example, "200 grams of cafeteria waste, including three apple cores, two banana peels, three orange peels, and three earthworms"). Keep a record of what happens to your compost in the chart below. Your measurement must include at least one number.

	Beginning	After 1 Week	After 2 Weeks	After 3 Weeks
Description				
Measurement				

What conclusions can you draw from observing your compost bin? Discuss the rate of decomposition in a compost bin—is it slow or fast?

_____

_____

_____

_____

How could you help take this project further at your school and/or at your home?

_____

_____

_____

_____

DON'T FORGET!

- Protective equipment, including but not limited to vinyl gloves, aprons, and eye goggles, is encouraged for the activities in this book.

- When working outdoors, students should be reminded not to look directly into the Sun.

For a full list of safety tips, see page xi.

Objective

Students will explore the heat produced by the Sun and the use of solar energy.

Topic: Heat Energy
Go to: www.scilinks.org
Code: BOS004

Why/How to Use This Lesson

Solar energy has become a viable energy alternative and is used in homes and businesses. Help students understand this through an exploration of the heat that the Sun can provide. If there is a window in your classroom that has exposure to the Sun, this will be the focal point of this lesson. The student activity would be best done on a sunny day.

Materials

thermometers, assorted small containers (boxes, cans, plastic containers), tape, construction paper (some should be black), paint, access to a window or a lamp, student worksheet

Procedures and Tips

1. Consider starting the lesson by placing a thermometer at a neutral point in the room, neither at the window nor near heating or air conditioning vents. Ask students to predict what the temperature is. After about 10 minutes, ask a student to check the temperature and have two more students serve as witnesses to verify the temperature.

2. In a class discussion, ask students to discuss the influences on the temperature in your classroom. Possible answers might be the outside temperature, heating or air conditioning, insulation, leaving the door open or closed, and the number of windows. Ask where it might be warmer, and guide students toward thinking about the window. Ask them how they could test this.

3. Divide the class into cooperative groups and give each group a thermometer. Allow them to use their thermometers to verify the temperature where the first thermometer was and then to move them to the windowsill. Have them record the temperatures on their worksheets.

4. Ask students how they might contain and harvest the heat energy, given a set of materials (boxes and other containers, paint, tape, construction paper, fabric, etc.).

5. Have students choose containers and give them the option to paint the the containers or cover them with paper. Encourage some discussion of color choice and the material the containers are made of. If no group chooses to paint a container black or to cover it in black paper, either suggest it or make one of your own and place a thermometer in it.

6. All groups should place their thermometer in their container and first record the temperature at the neutral spot in the room, and then move the thermometer to the window.

7. Students should record the temperature at the window at three or more 15-minute intervals. Hold a class discussion of the results. What do the results show us?

Grade-Level Considerations

For lower grades, it may be helpful to conduct this investigation as a whole class and simply discuss it with students. For older students, conducting this activity as a work group will give them the opportunity to consider the viewpoints of other students.

Assessment/Next Steps

The activity with the containers at the window may be repeated on another day so that students can gather and compare additional data.

(See also the lesson "The Sun and Its Impact on Earth" in Chapter 6.) Students could make a solar cooker following directions easily found on the internet (e.g., *http://solarcooking.org/plans*). One solar cooker uses a potato chip can to cook a hot-dog; others are boxes lined with aluminum foil. Another way to extend this lesson would be to order small solar panel kits from a reliable science vendor or look for them at a hobby store.

It is probably more effective to use solar cookers and panels outdoors, but a window with direct sunlight may be adequate.

Sample Discussion Questions

- How does sunlight affect the temperature of objects?
- How does the color of an object affect the temperature of the object?

USING SOLAR ENERGY

Name: _____ Date: _____

With your teacher and classmates in a small group, choose three locations and record the temperatures in your classroom.

Location	1	2	3
Temperature			

Work with your classmates to verify the temperatures you have recorded above, gathering data from other groups or students. List the group or student you got the information from.

Location	1	2	3
Temp. from _____			
Temp. from _____			
Temp. from _____			
Temp. from _____			

You may have found that the warmest spot in the room was in sunlight at a window. (If not, it was likely near a heater vent or other sources of warm air.) Test some different-color materials (paint, construction paper, fabric, etc.) to determine which one will retain the most heat in a container. Write down what you will do, adding more numbers for additional steps if you need to. Include taking a temperature reading at intervals.

1. _____
   _____
   _____

2. _____
   _____
   _____

3. _____
   _____
   _____

4. _____
   _____
   _____

What happened? What conclusions can you reach from your experiment?

_____
_____
_____

NATIONAL SCIENCE TEACHERS ASSOCIATION

DON'T FORGET!

- Provide students with a lab safety form or science activity safety form that outlines general science safety procedures. You can use your school system's standard form, if available. If you teach in an elementary school that does not use a standard form, check with a middle school science teacher. The safety form should be sent home to be signed by parents.

- Protective equipment, including but not limited to vinyl gloves, aprons, and eye goggles, is encouraged for the activities in this book.

- Use care when students are asked to use sharp objects (such as those in dissection kits, toothpicks, pipe cleaners, straight pins, rocks, or arrowheads).

For a full list of safety tips, see page xi.

Objective

Students will recognize measures to save electricity in their school and in their homes.

Topic: Alternative
Energy Resources
Go to: *www.scilinks.org*
Code: BOS005

Why/How to Use This Lesson

As students learn to become responsible consumers of electricity, they will need to know ways to save.

Materials

student worksheet, digital cameras or cell phone cameras (optional)

Procedures and Tips

1. Ask students to make a jot list of everything they can see from their seats in the classroom that uses electricity as a power source.

2. Facilitate a class discussion about electricity in schools and homes. Remind students that many objects use electricity by being charged (such as cell phones).

3. Give students the task of gathering information from all over the school regarding what uses electricity and any waste they see. In a middle school, students could take their worksheet with them throughout the day to record information. In an elementary school where students stay with one teacher all day, they can either take a tour of the school or make observations on the way to lunch, recess, and other activities.

4. Give students an opportunity to share what they have seen either as a whole class or in small groups. If they have seen excessive use of electricity, ask them to share possible solutions.

5. Share some information with students about alternative energy sources such as wind or solar energy. Ask how the school might take advantage of some of these resources.

Grade-Level Considerations

Consider making this a homework assignment for primary grade students so their parents can help them to list examples of places where electricity is not being used wisely. If you do this at school, you might want to make it a whole-group activity.

Assessment/Next Steps

Check the student worksheet for reasonable answers. Hold a class discussion to check for understanding. Consider inviting a guest speaker from your local power company or electric cooperative to discuss energy-saving measures and the process of providing electric power to an entire community.

Sample Discussion Questions

- What ways did you find that you could reduce the amount of electricity used?

- What differences are there in home and school that affect the ability to save energy/electricity?

SAVING ELECTRICITY

Name: _____ Date: _____

Make a jot list of everything you can see in your classroom that uses electricity.

_____

_____

_____

Find examples in your school of ways that electricity is being wasted and list them in the chart below, along with suggestions for energy savings.

Examples of Electricity Waste in School	Suggestions for Energy Savings

Find energy waste at home similar to what you have done in your school.

Examples of Electricity Waste at Home	Suggestions for Energy Savings

What forms of alternative energy can you name? Write two or three sentences to explain how each one gathers energy.

_____

_____

_____

Do some research on alternative energy resources. What possibilities might there be to use them at your home or school?

_____

_____

_____

Objective

Students will explore ways that water is used in their school and home and ways that it might be conserved.

Why/How to Use This Lesson

Topic: Water
Conservation

Go to: www.scilinks.org

Code: BOS006

Water conservation is important for many reasons, including the need to reduce the cost of treating water so that it is clean enough to use in our homes and schools and the need to prepare communities for water shortages (such as may occur during periods of drought). Students in elementary and middle school often study the water cycle, and an investigation like this one on water conservation would fit into those studies. (See also the "Measuring Water for a Day" lesson in Chapter 5.)

Materials

student worksheet, water collection containers for outdoors (optional)

Procedures and Tips

1. Ask students to think about ways that water is used in the school. You may want to give them a couple of days to make observations and add to a jot list.

2. Give students the opportunity to research ways that water can be conserved. You may want to conduct some prior research of your own using the internet or articles from newspapers or magazines.

3. After their research, ask students to list ways to conserve water beside each use on the chart for that area of the school.

4. Lead a whole-class discussion regarding water use and conservation, including ways that your class can contribute to water conservation in your school and community.

Grade-Level Considerations

As with the electricity lesson, you should consider making this a homework assignment for primary grade students. It can also be a whole-class activity.

Assessment/Next Steps

Discuss data that students have gathered either in small groups or as a class. If your school has plants that need to be watered (indoors or out), consider getting a rainwater collection barrel. Students could use the collected rainwater to water plants. If that's not possible, think of additional ways that water could be conserved, drawing from the lists that your students have made. Try to find at least one of the methods that can be implemented as an example in your school.

Sample Discussion Questions

• How can we contribute to water conservation in our school and community?

• Why is it important to conserve water resources?

SAVING WATER

Name: _____ Date: _____

How and where is water used in the school?

Place and Use of Water	Estimated Amount	Ways to Save Water (You may wait until after research and class discussion to fill in this section.)

Research some ways that people have tried to reduce the use of water. Make a bullet list of water-saving methods. Would any of these be helpful in your school?

- _____
- _____
- _____
- _____
- _____

Objective

Students will practice reusing simple objects for a new purpose.

Topic: Waste Management

Go to: www.scilinks.org

Code: BOS007

Why/How to Use This Lesson

As people become more reliant on instant satisfaction such as fast food, bottled water, and music downloads, they fill landfills with used items, packaging, and other waste. Creating a game with such items helps students look for ways to reuse items that they would normally discard. If the game has question cards or some other way that students must show their knowledge, it would be helpful to require that the questions be based on an environmental issue or facts about recycling.

Materials

empty pizza boxes, plastic bottle tops, discarded CDs, small boxes, and other discarded items; student worksheet

Procedures and Tips

1. Provide students with a number of discarded items such as those in the materials list and ask them to use these items to create a game that they would like to play. The game may have a theme related to reducing waste if you wish. Students may work in cooperative groups in order to foster creativity and reduce the amount of materials required.

2. Students should write the game instructions and rules, perhaps centering on recycling or environmental issues or facts.

3. Give students an opportunity to practice their game in the group that created it. If time allows, have students trade games with another group and give them a few minutes to play the game.

4. Games may be stored in the classroom and used as a sponge activity or learning center.

Grade-Level Considerations

To simplify this lesson for primary grade students, divide the materials into categories such as game boards and playing pieces. They can choose what they need from each set of materials. Parent volunteers could help students record the rules.

Assessment/Next Steps

Check game for having a high percentage of reused parts (100% if possible). Consider laminating the games and making them as durable as possible. Consider sharing these games with other teachers or with an after-school program, or sending them home with students.

Sample Discussion Questions

- (Ask this question before the activity while holding some discarded items that will be used in activity.) What are some ways we can reuse items like these?

- Describe how your game was able to reuse materials that would have been trash.

REUSE!

Name: _____ Date: _____

Can you use the materials provided by your teacher to make a game? Sure you can!

Games typically have certain parts. What materials will serve as these parts for your game?

Game pieces _____

Game board _____

Spinner or dice _____

Other _____

Write down the title of the game and the rules or instructions:

Title _____

Number of players _____

Instructions/Rules (add more numbers if needed):

1. _____
   _____

2. _____
   _____

3. _____
   _____

4. _____
   _____

5. _____
   _____

Objective
Students will lead recycling efforts in other classrooms throughout their grade level and/or school.

Topic: Recycling
Go to: www.scilinks.org
Code: BOS001

Why/How to Use This Lesson
Once students have learned some recycling basics, having the opportunity to put them into practice will reinforce their skills. Work with other teachers in your grade level or throughout your school to help make this happen. If taking on several classes is too much, you may want to partner with or adopt just one other class.

Materials
boxes or plastic containers that can hold recyclables, poster board, markers, student worksheet

Procedures and Tips
1. Get the support and participation of other teachers in your grade level or throughout the school, asking them to house recycling bins in their classrooms. Make sure that an administrator supports the recycling project.

2. Provide the resources to help students gather at least two types of recyclables so that comparative data may be gathered. As an alternative, gathering one item in at least two classrooms would work.

3. Ask your students to make recycling containers from boxes or label plastic bins if available. Match the number needed to the number of participating classrooms. Students should label them for whatever you intend to collect and recycle.

4. Use poster board to make a chart or list of which students are responsible for which classes. Depending on the grade level of your students, you may wish to give them input into these decisions.

5. Help students decide on which numbers to keep track of, such as how many cans or bottles are collected for recycling. Ask them to record data in a graph on their student worksheet.

Grade-Level Considerations
To adapt this lesson for lower grades, limit the number of items tracked to one or two and consider keeping all the records for your class. For upper grades increase the number of items, and require students to keep independent records.

Assessment/Next Steps
As students create their recycling program, consider how they are applying what they have learned. Have they included containers for the various materials that are recyclable? Consider comparing data from the participating classrooms. If possible, have students enter data into a computer program and create graphs or charts that show the amounts of materials that are recycled and how their collections compare with those of other classes.

Sample Discussion Questions
- What are some ways we can help teachers to recycle in their classrooms?
- How do students and teachers react to new recycling containers?

HELPING TEACHERS RECYCLE MORE

Name: _____ Date: _____

Make a jot list of any recyclable items that may be found at school, particularly what is found in classrooms or any items from lunches that students buy or bring.

_____
_____
_____

Work with your teacher to choose additional classrooms where teachers will participate in a recycling project. Gather at least two different types of recyclables for comparison, or one item from at least two classrooms. Keep a record of what is being recycled. The data should be numerical, either by weight, volume, or number of items (such as aluminum cans, plastic bottles, Styrofoam cups). Use the rectangle below to make a graph of your data. Gather the data each day for one week.

What was the total amount of recyclable material gathered?

_____

What was the difference between either two recycled items or two classrooms' recycled materials?

_____
_____

How much of this recyclable material could you gather in one month of school? How much in the whole school year?

_____
_____

Objectives

Students will apply recycling concepts learned at school to their homes. Students will identify recyclable materials and methods of recycling.

Topic: Recycling
Go to: www.scilinks.org
Code: BOS001

Why/How to Use This Lesson

While recycling at school is important, the bigger picture is making an impact on students that will last. If students can transfer what they have learned at school to another setting, it is possible to establish lifelong recycling habits. This lesson would best fit as an immediate follow-up to in-school lessons on recycling. If possible, consider kicking off a home recycling project near the time of a parent-teacher conference day or PTA meeting so that parents can be easily notified of the project.

Materials

student/parent worksheet, collection bags to send home (optional), large collection bins at school (optional)

Procedures and Tips

1. Gather data regarding which students and parents recycle in their home. (Optional: Create a paper or online survey for parents to gather more details on what items are recycled.)

2. Regardless of the level of recycling at home, encourage students to choose one recyclable item to focus on that is not currently part of any home recycling projects. This does not have to be a consistent item throughout the class, just one item per home.

3. If you have some students who do not have support from home for this project, consider pairing them with another student, or start a recycling project at your home and let those students track the data for your items. You

may wish to involve other adults in the school for a variety of data.

4. As a class, make a jot list of some of the items that you have learned about that are recyclable. As students are thinking about items that are not recycled at home, help them to be realistic and choose an item that is manageable. For instance, used car parts or large electronics might not work.

5. When possible, encourage students to choose a recyclable item that can easily be counted (aluminum cans, newspapers, tin cans, plastic bottles, glass jars, etc.).

6. Give students the worksheet and discuss using this at home to gather data.

Grade-Level Considerations

Consider pairing up primary grade students with an upper-grade class so the older students can help the younger students.

Assessment/Next Steps

Follow up with parents at a PTA meeting or open house. Work within your community to establish a recycling day at your school. Some electronics retailers may be willing to sponsor an electronics recycling day for old computers, televisions, and similar items. If this is not possible, find information on recycling events or recycling collection centers to put in a class newsletter or on a class website. Encourage parents to involve your students in recycling at home.

Sample Discussion Questions

- How could we encourage parents to recycle?
- Why are people sometimes resistant to recycling?

ENCOURAGING RECYCLING AT HOME

Name: _____ Date: _____

Make a jot list of items that could be recycled in a home.
_____
_____

Find out about an item that is not currently recycled at your home (or that of a classmate) that can be recycled/recyclable. List one item for which you will attempt to track recycling.

_____

List how many of the recyclable items are recycled each day for a period of one week.

	Monday	Tuesday	Wednesday	Thursday	Friday	Saturday	Sunday	TOTAL
Number of Items Recycled								

If possible, use a bathroom scale to weigh the items. (Weigh yourself holding a bag first, and then put the recyclable items in the bag. The additional weight will be the weight of the items.) Record the weight of your items.

_____

Figure out how much trash could be prevented from going to landfills by recycling this item for one month and for one year.

One month _____   One year _____

Compare your data for a month and a year with that of a classmate who kept track of a different item. If you could only choose one of the two to recycle, which one would save more weight from a landfill? How much weight could be prevented from going into the landfill if both were recycled for one year?

_____
_____
_____
_____

25

Objectives

Students will collect litter or debris in their community and discover how it may harm wildlife and the environment. Students will practice creative writing skills.

Topic: Pollution
Go to: www.scilinks.org
Code: BOS008

Why/How to Use This Lesson

To become good environmental stewards, students must learn to care for the natural surroundings in their own communities.

Projects that need community volunteers include but are not limited to river cleanups, seashore debris collection, and roadside litter collection. Either tap into an existing community cleanup activity or plan and execute one of your own. Students may serve as volunteers, and it may be helpful to get parents involved too.

Consider starting on the school grounds by picking up any litter or unwanted materials in the school yard, school parking lot, or playground. Students can write about some of the items you have gathered, and as a follow-up students can pick up litter and write about one of the items they collect. If it is not possible to have students to collect litter, you may simply use items that you have collected or clip art of litter.

You may want to focus on an animal that is native to your area, asking students to think about how certain garbage items provide challenges to that animal. For instance, many animals will try to eat plastic grocery bags, while others might get tangled in the plastic rings from a six-pack of soda cans.

Materials

debris items you have collected *or* clip art/ photographs of litter, collection bags, work gloves (or any type of gloves that would protect hands), student worksheet

Procedures and Tips

1. Consider using actual debris items you have collected from an area in your community. An alternative would be to use clean trash items you have saved or photographs of these items.

2. Give an item to each student or to a small cooperative group of students. You may also consider having three objects displayed in the classroom and asking students to choose one that is of interest. Some items that may work well are the plastic rings from the top of a soda six-pack, a plastic jar, a plastic grocery bag, or any other unbreakable item with no sharp edges.

3. Ask the students to consider how these items would end up in a natural habitat instead of the recycling bin, and also how these items might harm area wildlife. Depending on their grade or ability level, ask students to write a few sentences, paragraph, or a paper about how the item came to be in a natural setting and how it may have interfered with the health or well-being of an animal.

4. If the students are just writing a couple of sentences, you may wish to have them read sentences out loud, or put them on sentence strips to be posted on a bulletin board with the debris item attached. For older students writing a paper, you may wish to have them share an oral synopsis of their story after it is completed.

Grade-Level Considerations

For primary grade students, instead of having them write on a worksheet consider keeping a class list on chart paper. You can also lead your younger students in a school yard cleanup. They can pick up litter and place it in proper trash receptacles or recycling bins.

Assessment/Next Steps

Check sentences or paragraphs for understanding, in particular to see if the student makes the connection between litter and harm to animals and the environment. If possible, get some information on local cleanup efforts and send it to parents. If you have a class website, post links to organizations that sponsor river cleanups, roadside litter collection, and similar activities.

Sample Discussion Questions

- What are some ways that we could help to improve our community's natural resources?
- Where are areas in our community that could be improved by a cleanup effort?

COMMUNITY CLEANUP PROJECT

Name: _____ Date: _____

Look at these examples of writing about how litter affects wildlife and the environment:

- "When the turtle took a bite out of the plastic milk container, he was unaware that it could make him feel sick."
- "When the raccoon licked the antifreeze that had leaked on to the driveway, there was no way to know this sweet-tasting liquid could make her sick."
- "With a wing stuck in the broken kite that hung from the power line, there was no way the bird could escape on its own."

Think about a piece of litter that you have seen—either provided by your teacher, in a photograph, or from your efforts to clean up a natural setting. Consider how it might be harmful to wildlife and write the beginning of a story below, following teacher directions for the number of sentences.

_____

_____

_____

_____

Draw a sketch of the item you have written about. List three ways the item could have been recycled or reused instead of becoming litter.

INSECTS

2

I f for no other reason than their sheer numbers, insects warrant a chapter in a book on outdoor science. Many species of insects have survived for millions of years, and in some ways remain unchanged. They are a real success story in the natural world. When working in a science classroom or school yard, the advantages of teaching lessons on insects are numerous. When teachers are strapped for funding, it's often easy to catch a cricket or a butterfly for students to observe as opposed to purchasing a critter at a pet store or ordering living samples from a science supplier. Another advantage is the size. As small as they can be, insects exhibit many of the behaviors of other members of the animal kingdom, and are often a reasonable portrayal of relationships in nature such as predator/prey.

It is possible for students to observe insects in the school yard without even catching them. A pollination garden draws in bees and butterflies and allows students to make observations about animal behavior and the relationship between flowering plants and insects. If it is not possible to go outside, carnivorous plants like a Venus flytrap can be purchased and placed in a classroom for another example of animal/plant relationships. There are even kits available from science suppliers that will bring plants and pollinators into the classroom in an inclusive package. Either indoors or out, there are multiple ways to make sure students see insects in action.

Use the lessons in this chapter to shape a unit on insects or to support instruction in a larger instructional unit on animals. Creating a "bug zoo" in your classroom gives students opportunities to see animal behaviors over a period of time, and perhaps even to design their own experiments and draw parallels between insects and other animals. At the very least, it may help students gain a greater appreciation for insects and make them think twice before succumbing to the human urge to immediately destroy insects on sight.

Depending on your state standards and school district parameters, you'll need to decide between teaching a unit on insects that would include all of these lessons or pulling a few lessons out to support other big ideas or units of instruction. Some of the lessons lend themselves to the study of animal relationships, such as "Predators of Insects." The study of ecosystems would be incomplete without lessons on food webs and food chains, and the "Insect Food Chain" lesson would work well for that purpose. Taken as a group, these lessons could anchor an insect unit and could be supported with additional information from the websites and children's literature selections listed below.

Safety Notes

1. Make sure not to bring stinging insects indoors, and do not allow students to handle them during outdoor observations.

2. Do not substitute other animals for insects in these activities.

3. Spiders for classroom use should be nonvenomous.

Resources

Websites

- *www.ars.usda.gov/is/kids*
- *www.discoveryeducation.com/teachers/free-lesson-plans/the-insect-world.cfm*
- *www.monarchwatch.org*
- *www.orkin.com/learningcenter/kids_and_teachers_lessonplans.aspx*

Children's Literature

Bug Zoo by Nick Baker (DK Publishing, 2010)

DON'T FORGET!

- Review students' records for allergies such as those to specific plants or stinging insects.
- When gathering any objects outdoors (rocks, soil, insects, etc.), it is best to look for locations that have not been sprayed with pesticides, herbicides, or other chemicals.
- When working outdoors, students should be reminded not to look directly into the Sun.

For a full list of safety tips, see page xi.

Objectives

Students will record their observations about insects. Students will accurately describe an insect and its parts, including six legs and other distinguishing features such as antennae, wings, and large eyes.

SCI LINKS
THE WORLD'S A CLICK AWAY
Topic: Insects
Go to: *www.scilinks.org*
Code: BOS009

Why/How to Use This Lesson

Lessons on insects help students develop an understanding of the place that insects hold in the natural world and how they help humans. Often the first reaction to an insect encounter is to kill the insect rather than let it be. The common misconception that all insects are harmful to humans may be at the root of this reaction, so it is important to address the misconception.

Materials

live insects, clear plastic containers, hand lens, student handout, *Bug Zoo* (optional; see the "Resources" section at the beginning of this chapter), digital camera or photos downloaded from the internet (optional)

Procedures and Tips

During a unit on insects, it may be helpful to your students to create a temporary bug zoo in the classroom. The book *Bug Zoo* gives step-by-step instructions on how to do this; consult that book if you need details beyond what is provided in this lesson. Students can create an insect container that they can take home. They can also create the containers needed for your classroom zoo, or you can buy "critter containers" at a local pet store or discount store.

1. You can take students outdoors to capture insects, or you can purchase insects from a science vendor's catalog. Insects such as praying mantis, ladybug beetle, butterfly larva/chrysalis, and hissing cockroaches are often available through reputable science vendors.

2. Have one insect in a container in your classroom at the start of the unit. It may be as simple as a grasshopper found in the school yard and released at the end of the day.

3. Show the insect to your class. If possible, take some digital photos and project them on a screen or whiteboard, or use photos from the internet depicting the type of insect you have. If you have enough materials and insects, provide about six containers of insects so that students can work in small groups to observe the insect. Get one-word descriptions of the insect from as many students as possible.

4. While students are calling out words, ask each student to make a jot list of the words.

5. Facilitate a discussion of the various descriptive words and discuss how they might be placed into categories. Give students the worksheet with the columns and have them create three categories to place the words in.

   Optional step: Use poster board or a projection on a whiteboard to make a class chart.

6. Ask students how having this list would help a scientist who studies insects. The purpose of this discussion is to get students to realize that the descriptive words are the record of observations—the same types of observations that scientists make and that help them gather evidence.

7. Talk to students about the study of insects that you are beginning with this lesson, and tell them that observations will be very important in this study.

Grade-Level Considerations

For primary grades, see step 5 on previous page.

Assessment/Next Steps

Check jot lists to see if students have accurately described the insect; this will determine if they have grasped the ability to record what they see. After this lesson, students could compare the insect characteristics on their lists with those of a different insect in order to understand that there are many different kinds of insects and that only general characteristics are the same (six legs, compound eyes, etc.).

Sample Discussion Questions

- What words would you use to describe an insect?

- What do insects need in order to survive?

BUG ZOO

Name: _____ Date: _____

Take a close look at a live insect that your teacher provides. Make a jot list of words that describe an insect you observe, and create three categories to put these words into.

How would a scientist use this list to classify insects?

_____

_____

_____

Compare the insect you observed with a different one. What words are in your jot list that you could not use for the different insect?

_____

_____

_____

Use the space below to make a sketch of the insect(s) you observed.

DON'T FORGET!

- Provide students with a lab safety form or science activity safety form that outlines general science safety procedures. You can use your school system's standard form, if available. If you teach in an elementary school that does not use a standard form, check with a middle school science teacher. The safety form should be sent home to be signed by parents.

- Students should thoroughly wash their hands after any visits to the school yard and after handling any materials that have been taken in from outdoors.

For a full list of safety tips, see page xi.

Objective

Students will make observations about animal behavior and record and interpret their data.

Topic: Behavior
Go to: www.scilinks.org
Code: BOS010

Why/How to Use This Lesson

As the largest group of animals on the planet, insects are representative of animal behavior of many species. Students can learn from insect behavior and make generalizations about all animals. From this, they can begin to understand many of the adaptations that animals have made over time.

Materials

live insects, clear containers, materials for measuring how insects fit through openings in objects (optional), student worksheet

Procedures and Tips

1. You can take students outdoors to capture insects, or you can purchase insects from a science vendor's catalog. Insects such as praying mantis, ladybug beetle, butterfly larva/chrysalis, and hissing cockroaches are often available through reputable science vendors.

2. Students can make their observations of insects that are in clear critter containers.

3. To make this activity an inquiry experience for students, teachers should leave some of the decisions on how to experiment in the hands of students. Perhaps give some examples, but allow students to make the final determination. One possibility would be to observe how insects fit through tiny openings in objects and measure the openings in centimeters or millimeters. Another set of observations could be made by giving the insects more than one type of food and trying to determine if there is any preference for one or the other.

4. Data can be recorded with tally marks and then placed in a graph.

Grade-Level Considerations

The student worksheet is not needed when teaching this lesson to primary grades. The teacher can keep one graph for the class on chart paper and ask for observations of one particular behavior. For instance, if the students are observing crickets or grasshoppers, ask them to count the number of times the insect hops in a two-minute period.

Assessment/Next Steps

Evaluate the students' graphs and numerical data. If possible, hold individual conferences so that each student can explain the meaning of the information in the graph. Consider pairing or grouping students who have gathered similar data. It may be possible to compile information from several students' graphs into one, perhaps using a computer projector or poster board to share with the entire class.

Sample Discussion Questions

• What do you see your insect doing? Why is the insect doing this?

• What types of behaviors do insects repeat? Why?

OBSERVING INSECT BEHAVIOR

Name: _____ Date: _____

Insects exhibit a variety of behaviors. Gather some numerical data about one of the behaviors you see. Which one would you like to observe? What do you expect to see?

_____

_____

_____

_____

Use the box below to create a graph using data you have gathered about insect behavior.

What does your graph mean? What conclusions can you draw from the data?

_____

_____

_____

_____

INSECT FOOD CHAIN

Objective

Students will create and observe an animal habitat that contains at least two different insects, one predator and one prey.

Topic: Food Chains
Go to: *www.scilinks.org*
Code: BOS011

Why/How to Use This Lesson

Many members of the insect family eat other insects. There are other predators as well, but for the purpose of this activity we will focus on insects that prey on other insects.

Materials

live predator and prey insects such as praying mantis and cricket, clear plastic containers, student worksheet

Procedures and Tips

1. Determine which insects you will use for your students' habitats. Some insects may be gathered in the school yard, or you can order them from a reputable science supply vendor.

2. Obtain enough clear plastic containers in which students can create the insect habitat. Large plastic jars may be available from restaurants or your school cafeteria once the food inside them has been used. You may also purchase "critter containers" at pet stores.

3. Scout out locations in the school yard where students might observe an insect food chain in action, and take a trip outside as a class if possible. Another option is to have one teacher-created food chain habitat in a container in the classroom.

4. Students should be given a few minutes to observe the food chain. If it's in a container in the classroom, it may be helpful to have it there a few days so that students can take turns looking at it. Students should use the information gathered in the observations to complete the worksheet.

Grade-Level Considerations

Younger students may be upset by one insect eating another, so for primary grades consider using caterpillars (which eat leaves instead of insects). Rather than use the worksheet, ask students to draw what they see and label the food and the insect.

Assessment/Next Steps

Check student answers on the worksheet for understanding, including the use of insect predators to control pests on plants (e.g., releasing ladybugs to eat aphids that attack ornamental or agricultural plants). In addition to using containers to observe insect predators in the classroom, there may be opportunities to watch them in action outdoors. You can also create an observation opportunity outdoors; for example, some science supply companies sell ladybugs that can be safely released to control aphids.

Sample Discussion Questions

- What types of food do insects eat?
- Describe what might happen if insects stopped eating insects and the remains of other animals.

38

NATIONAL SCIENCE TEACHERS ASSOCIATION

INSECT FOOD CHAIN

Name: _____ Date: _____

Energy Source	Plant
Insect 1	Insect 2

Fill in the boxes above with sketches showing a food chain that contains two insects. Label each insect (for example, cricket and praying mantis) and the plant material (onion, potato, milkweed, etc.).

Does the insect that is prey have any defense? How is this situation different from the natural habitat?

_____

_____

_____

_____

_____

2

Objective

Students will examine insects as prey for other types of animals.

SC/LINKS®
THE WORLD'S A CLICK AWAY

Topic: Predator/Prey
Go to: www.scilinks.org
Code: BOS012

Why/How to Use This Lesson

The predator/prey relationship is an important component of any ecosystem. In addition to using this lesson during a unit on insects, consider using it when teaching about ecosystems, food webs, and food chains.

Materials

sets of live insects (e.g., crickets or grasshoppers) and their predators (e.g., a small turtle, nonvenomous snake, or nonvenomous spider) or video clips of insects as prey for other animals; clear containers; student worksheet

Procedures and Tips

1. Gather sets of live insects and their predators (crickets or grasshoppers, snake, turtle, spider). As an alternative, you can use video clips of insects as prey, or possibly make these observations outdoors.

2. Set up containers where students can observe the predator in action.

3. Students can take notes in a science notebook or journal detailing what they observe. Students may use the worksheet to consider the predator/prey relationship.

4. Allow students to discuss their observations in small groups, and then hold a class discussion of the observations.

Grade-Level Considerations

Younger students may be upset by one insect eating another, so for primary grades consider using caterpillars (which eat leaves instead of insects).

Assessment/Next Steps

If you have an aquarium or class pet in your classroom, you may have the perfect setup for showing the predator/prey relationship beyond this lesson. If not, this may be the time to consider a classroom animal that eats other living things. For instance, some nonvenomous snakes can eat crickets or minnows. Spiders can eat crickets, as can turtles. Many pet stores sell "feeder" crickets or small fish. After setting up an observation of the predator/prey relationship in your classroom, you should encourage students to make other observations in nature, or you can show video clips from web streaming or another source. School yard nature walks or field trips to a zoo are good follow-ups.

Sample Discussion Questions

- What animals eat insects? Why are insects a good food for these animals?

- Do insects ever eat other insects? What are the benefits to the environment as a result?

PREDATORS OF INSECTS

Name: _____ Date: _____

Observe the container provided. Which animal is the predator?

_____

What reaction does it have to the insect in the habitat? Describe in terms of speed, movement, visibility, etc.

_____

_____

_____

What advantages and disadvantages does this predator have for preying on insects?

_____

_____

_____

How can humans use these predatory relationships to an advantage?

_____

_____

_____

What other types of animals are predators of insects?

_____

_____

Make a jot list of living things that can be in a food web. Include at least two insects.

_____

_____

Use the back of this page to draw a food web that includes the living things in your jot list. You may add others.

Objective

Students will distinguish among three invertebrates and determine the characteristics that make each one unique.

Topic: Invertebrates
Go to: www.scilinks.org
Code: BOS013

Why/How to Use This Lesson

Students come into contact with small creatures in everyday life. Helping students understand the niche that each creature has in the environment can change the tendency to immediately stomp on or otherwise kill spiders, insects, and worms. This lesson might serve as an introduction to animal classification. In this case, discuss misconceptions such as lumping small creatures under common words such as "bugs" or believing that all insects are harmful to humans.

Materials

live spider, earthworm, and insect; hand lens; student worksheet

Procedures and Tips

1. Provide students with live specimens to observe. These may be earthworms, spiders, and insects that you bring in from outdoors. Be sure that you are familiar with species of spiders and know that the type you have is safe.

2. Keep the specimens in separate containers. You could set up a station for students to visit with each creature and take notes. If you have enough of each (spider, earthworm,

and insect), then you could have three small containers at each table or group of four to five students. Either way, provide several minutes for students to watch each of the animals.

3. Students can take detailed notes in a science notebook or journal and then record information on the student worksheet, or they can write directly on the worksheet.

4. Lead a class discussion on the similarities and differences in the species. Ask students how each animal is adapted to its environment.

Grade-Level Considerations

For primary grades, consider using two instead of three of the creatures for this lesson.

Assessment/Next Steps

If this lesson is used as an introduction to classification, it may be helpful to follow up with a similar look at plants or larger animals. If it is not possible to look at living examples of larger animals, use photographs or internet art of other animals to make cards that can be sorted according to their characteristics. A field trip to a zoo, aquarium, or wildlife park can also be a good followup; students can make written observations and create tables and charts to organize their data.

Sample Discussion Questions

How are these three animals alike? How are they different?

WHAT'S THE DIFFERENCE BETWEEN A SPIDER, AN EARTHWORM, AND AN INSECT?

Name: _____ Date: _____

Use the chart below to list traits of each animal:

Spider	Earthworm	Insect

Choose one of these three animals to sketch below:

In your opinion, what are the three most distinguishing features of the animal you have chosen to sketch?

_____

_____

_____

_____

_____

Objective

Students will compare and contrast how insects move.

Topic: Characteristics
of Living Things

Go to: www.scilinks.org

Code: BOS014

Why/How to Use This Lesson

One of the characteristics of many living things is the ability to move. How insects move helps them survive life in the ecosystems in which they live. Insects that fly may have access to a larger environment than those that hop, and those that hop may be able to cover a greater area than those that only walk. Helping students learn about how animals and insects move will help them better understand many types of animal adaptations. Students will also be able to use important process skills such as observation and measurement.

Materials

live insects or video clips of insects, tape measure or meterstick, student worksheet

Procedures and Tips

1. Provide opportunities for students to view live insects or video clips of insects moving around (flying, hopping, walking). You can provide containers with live specimens to individual students or small groups, or you can set up an activity center with streaming video from the internet for the whole class. Some of the insects that might be helpful to illustrate various modes of movement are ants (walking), grasshoppers or crickets (hopping), and bees or butterflies (flying).

2. Ask students to record their observations in a science notebook or journal, and if using live insects, to take measurements if possible.

3. Generate a class discussion of what the insect's purpose is in movement. Is it to find food, avoid predators, or some other purpose? The goal of this discussion is to lead students to discover some of the purposes insects serve in ecosystems, such as pollination or consumption and removal of decaying organisms.

4. Students can use the chart on the worksheet to organize information, relying on notes from their science journals or notebooks.

Grade-Level Considerations

For primary grades, instead of using the chart divide students into three groups. Ask them to make the motions of flying, hopping, or walking to represent different types of insect movement.

Assessment/Next Steps

Assess students on reasonable answers on the worksheet. If students did not get to see a variety of insect movements in their observations, they may need to gather additional information from the internet or a resource book.

Sample Discussion Questions

Why do insects move in different ways? What advantages does this give them?

FLY, HOP, OR WALK?

2

Name: _____ Date: _____

List insects that move each way in the chart.

Walk	Hop	Fly

What visible physical differences are there in an insect that flies compared with one that hops? How do these differences help the insect?

_____
_____
_____
_____

Why is it beneficial to an ecosystem to have insects that move/travel in different ways?

_____
_____
_____
_____

Why do insects that can fly and/or hop need to be able to walk as well?

_____
_____
_____
_____

What would a "super" insect look like that could move in all three ways? What advantages would this insect have?

_____
_____
_____
_____

Objective

Students will recognize (and observe if possible) the important role insects play in the decomposition of organic material.

Topic: Decomposers
Go to: *www.scilinks.org*
Code: BOS015

Why/How to Use This Lesson

Insects play a major role in decomposition of living things, which is an important concept for students to know and understand. For instance, if a large tree or a large wild animal dies, insects speed up the process of decomposition. Opportunities to share this may arise as part of a unit on energy transfer or ecosystems.

Materials

clear plastic containers of live insects and organic materials that they consume (e.g., potato and mealworm, a piece of rotting log, or assorted fruit and vegetable waste for compost), scale, tape measure, digital camera (optional), student worksheet

Procedures and Tips

1. Obtain some organic material that an insect can eat, such as a rotting log, potatoes, or other fruits and vegetables. Have two samples of the material, one that will be eaten and one that can serve as a control. (Note: The rest of the procedure assumes that potatoes are used.)

2. Guide students through the process of weighing and measuring the potatoes. They should also take digital photographs if possible to document the original condition of the potatoes.

3. Obtain mealworms from a reputable science vendor or a local bait shop, and put them in a clear container with one of the potatoes. Cut it in half to give insects access to the inside of the potato.

4. Put the other potato in the same type of container as the first one, but with no insects.

5. Ask students to make predictions as to what will happen to the two potatoes. How will they change over time? Ask how they can gather evidence. (They should reach the conclusion that evidence can be gathered by taking digital photographs or by measuring with the tape measure and weighing the potatoes with the scale.)

6. Students should notice that the insects expedite the process of decomposition, and they should record this information on the student worksheet or in a science journal or notebook.

7. Allow at least a couple of weeks to follow the decomposition. During this time and near the conclusion of the observations, facilitate discussions of how insects aid in speeding up the decomposition process of organic material after an organism has died.

Grade-Level Considerations

For primary grades, keep a class chart instead of individual charts.

Assessment/Next Steps

Assess for reasonable responses on the worksheet. Consider locating a rotting log in the school yard. Allow students to take digital photographs at intervals to document changes that take place. If it is not possible to do this outdoors, some science equipment vendors sell a small piece of a rotting log in a container that can be kept in a classroom.

Sample Discussion Questions

- What would happen if insects didn't eat rotting animals or plants?

- Is there a daily difference in plant items left for insects to eat? Explain.

HOW INSECTS HELP HUMANS

Name: _____ Date: _____

Gather evidence that documents the original state of the organic material your teacher has asked you to observe (potato or other vegetable/fruit). Use whatever is available—scale, tape measure or ruler, camera, or simply your own observations and notes. Record your data here:

_____
_____
_____

Make some predictions. How will the sample of organic material change if left at room temperature in a container for one week? Two weeks? More?

_____
_____
_____

What would change if insects were added to the container holding the organic materials?

_____
_____
_____

Find out if your predictions were correct. Record what you see in the chart below and include additional notes on the back of this sheet or in a science journal or notebook.

	Visual Description	Weight	Length and/or Width
Week 1			
Day 1			
Day 3			
Day 5			
Week 2			
Day 1			
Day 3			
Day 5			
Week 3 (Conclusion)			

Notes and observations:

PLANTS AS A HABITAT FOR INSECTS

Objective

Students will recognize the important role that plants play in providing both habitats and food sources for insects.

Topic: Habitats
Go to: www.scilinks.org
Code: BOS016

Why/How to Use This Lesson

Habitat destruction is one of the major causes of endangerment of wildlife, including insects. Certain insects have very specific needs that can only be met by particular types of plants. Helping young students understand these concepts is important to their development as stewards of the Earth and scientifically literate citizens.

Materials

milkweed plants and monarch caterpillars *or* Wisconsin Fast Plants and cabbage butterfly larva, terrarium (optional), flowerpot with netting (optional), student worksheet

Procedures and Tips

1. Choose a plant to have in your classroom that serves as a host to butterflies, such as milkweed, thistle, or Wisconsin Fast Plants.

2. Secure the animal that lives on the plant and have one or more of them on the plant. One option would be to place the plant in a terrarium with a top so the insects cannot escape. Another option is to put a sleeve of netting over the plant in a flowerpot. If possible, you may wish to keep the plant

outdoors without a cover, particularly if the intention is for students to see the plant and insects as they would exist in a natural setting.

3. Give students opportunities to observe the plant habitat for insects and to record their observations on the student worksheet or in a science journal or notebook.

4. Once students have had several opportunities to make observations, facilitate a class discussion to report findings and conclusions from what the students have seen and recorded.

Grade-Level Considerations

For primary grades, instead of using the worksheet ask the students to draw and label a picture of the plant and insects.

Assessment/Next Steps

Assess student observations recorded on the worksheets or in science journals for reasonable entries. Note whether or not students make the connection that the plant and animal both benefit from the relationship. To follow up on this lesson, students may reflect on life on a larger plant by using the activity "The Story of Life in a Tree" from *Outdoor Science: A Practical Guide* (Rich 2010).

Sample Discussion Questions

- Why are plants so important to insects?
- How do insects help plants? How do insects hurt plants?

PLANTS AS A HABITAT FOR INSECTS

Name: _____ Date: _____

What type of plant are you observing? _____

Which insect(s) call this plant home?

_____

Use the chart below to organize your observations according to your teacher's instructions.

Date	What are the insects doing?	What observations can you make about the plant?

How does the plant help the insect?

_____

_____

How does the insect help the plant?

_____

_____

Objective

Students will recognize the various stages of insect metamorphosis and the advantages of metamorphosis.

Topic: Metamorphosis
Go to: www.scilinks.org
Code: BOS017

Why/How to Use This Lesson

Students need to understand the benefits of having a life cycle. The primary benefit is that there is not competition for the same food source for two stages of life (e.g., caterpillars, the larval stage of butterflies, eat leaves; butterflies [i.e., adult stage] drink nectar.) The needs of each stage in the life cycle allow for a variety of other needs to be met, such as getting plenty of food during the larval stage and lots of rest during the pupal stage.

Materials

live insects in various stages of their life cycle (or use photographs), student worksheet

Procedures and Tips

1. Discuss the advantages and disadvantages of metamorphosis with your class. Use the live insects or photographs to generate discussion points, and ask students to make lists on their worksheets of the advantages and disadvantages.

2. Ask students to sketch and label three or four stages of an insect life cycle depending on what photographs or living insects are available for observations.

Grade-Level Considerations

Students in primary grades can draw pictures of the stages of metamorphosis. The chart can be done as a class instead of on the student worksheet.

Assessment/Next Steps

Assess student understanding by checking for a reasonable list of advantages and disadvantages. Check the sketches and labels to see that they are representative of the insects or photographs provided. Following this lesson, you may wish to have students compare and contrast insect metamorphosis with that of another animal such as a frog by using additional live specimens or photographs from the internet or another source.

Sample Discussion Questions

- How do animals change as they grow?
- What are the advantages of metamorphosis? Explain.

INSECT METAMORPHOSIS

Name: _____ Date: _____

List the advantages and disadvantages of metamorphosis in the chart below:

Advantages	Disadvantages

Make a sketch of each phase of the life cycle of an insect based on photographs or live specimens. Each insect should have at least three phases, and some will have four.

Did the insect you sketched have complete or incomplete metamorphosis? What is the difference?

_____

_____

_____

_____

Objectives

Students will practice gathering data by estimating how many plants a pollinator can visit in a given amount of time. Students will explore the role of pollinators in the ecosystem.

Topic: Pollination
Go to: *www.scilinks.org*
Code: BOS018

Why/How to Use This Lesson

The exploration of pollinators' roles in the environment provides an opportunity to highlight the mutualistic relationship between plants and animals and to practice gathering and reporting data on pollination. It is important for students to understand that many insects and other creatures that may be seen as a nuisance or pests have a valuable role in the ecosystem. Additionally, many students who have been taught to kill a bee on sight because bees can sting don't realize that a bee will not bother a human unless provoked or disturbed.

Materials

Wisconsin Fast Plants Kit and pollination wand *or* other small flowering plant and cotton swabs, video clips of flower pollination, student worksheet

Procedures and Tips

1. Provide an opportunity for students to observe natural or manual pollination of flowers, on video, outdoors in a school garden, or with Wisconsin Fast Plants. If using Wisconsin Fast Plants, the kits come with a "bee stick" (pollination wand) which students may use to simulate pollination. It is similar in size to a cotton swab, which may be used in its place.

2. Ask students to use the worksheet to gather information on what they see in the plants.

3. Regardless of whether the pollination is natural or manual, the important aspect of the lesson is for students to record numerical data and draw conclusions from the information that is pertinent.

Grade-Level Considerations

Students in primary grades can model pollination with paper cutouts of flowers, pollen, and bees. You may also wish to use puppets for this.

Assessment/Next Steps

Check student worksheet for appropriate data and conclusions. If the students have observed pollination indoors, ideally they should be given an opportunity to go outdoors and look for pollinators in nature. Consider inviting a guest speaker such as a botanist or entomologist to discuss the role of insects in pollination.

Sample Discussion Questions

- Why is it important not to kill bees?
- How does pollen move from one plant to another?

POLLINATION NATION

Name: _____ Date: _____

Use the chart below to organize data regarding the pollination you have observed or manually created. You may add lines to further divide the chart if necessary. Organize data as you choose, recording each pollination event for each plant, or some other way that is representative of what you have seen.

How could scientists use data similar to what you have gathered to further study pollination?

_____
_____
_____
_____
_____

Why is pollination so important in nature? How would an area change if no pollination took place for a year?

_____
_____
_____
_____

Objective

Students will investigate the benefits of exoskeletons through building models.

Topic: Insects
Go to: www.scilinks.org
Code: BOS009

Why/How to Use This Lesson

In a unit on insects, there is often discussion but rarely experimentation with what it is like to have an exoskeleton. Students can benefit from modeling with objects that can simulate the exoskeleton of an insect.

Materials

hard, curved materials for exoskeleton models (e.g., hard plastic bowls or cups, plastic Easter eggs, plastic bottles), items for model legs (e.g., toothpicks, plastic utensils), objects for antennae (e.g., pipe cleaners), bicycle or military helmets, material to stuff pillows or bag of cotton balls, rock (optional), student worksheet

Procedures and Tips

1. Demonstrate for students how an exoskeleton provides strength from outside by turning a small hard plastic bowl or cup upside down and then balancing a much heavier item on top of it such as a couple of textbooks or a rock.

2. Ask students to describe what they see. Question whether or not an object must have a hard internal structure in order to support something heavy. Bring students around to whether or not this applies to living things, and discuss what gives the human body structure. Generate discussion about the difference between human skeletons and insect skeletons.

3. Ask students what materials they might use to model an exoskeleton. Allow students to select materials from a variety of common objects such as empty bottles, plastic eggs, helmets, etc.

4. To simulate soft tissue, you may wish to have some stuffing (similar to what is used in pillows) or a bag of cotton balls. If you are using a bag of cotton balls, put them under a helmet or an upside-down bowl and place a heavy book on top. Then lay the cotton balls on a desk or table and put the book directly on them. Ask students which condition will damage soft tissue.

Grade-Level Considerations

For primary grades, consider a "dress-up" activity where students wear helmets or other materials that would simulate an exoskeleton.

Assessment/Next Steps

Check student models of exoskeletons and discuss with individuals or small groups how their model is similar to and different from a real exoskeleton. As a follow-up, keep some live insects in a habitat container in the classroom and ask students to make observations and take notes in a science notebook or journal on how the insects' exoskeletons aid in survival.

Sample Discussion Questions

- How does your skeleton help you?
- What would it be like if your skeleton was on the outside of your body?

WEARING A SKELETON ON THE OUTSIDE

Name: _____ Date: _____

What are the characteristics and advantages of skeletons?

Exoskeleton	Endoskeleton	Both

What would happen to an insect with no skeleton? _____
_____
_____

What would happen to a human with no skeleton? _____
_____
_____

Make a sketch of your exoskeleton model. Write three sentences to describe it.

_____
_____
_____
_____
_____

PLANTS

3

Life on Earth as we know it is dependent on plants. Some types of plants have been around for millions of years, recycling the oxygen that is needed to keep animals alive. Plants provide humans with a source of food, shelter, medication, and sometimes fuel. For some animals, a single plant is their complete habitat for a lifetime, which speaks to the importance of plants. To think that a single plant can provide everything another living thing needs is astounding. For example, some insects can ingest all of the water needed to survive by eating plant leaves.

Because of the wide range of characteristics and the important roles of plants, it is important for students to learn about them. Students in elementary and middle school should have opportunities to get their hands on seeds, fruit, flowers, and all parts of a plant. They should be given the chance to experiment with various ways to grow plants, and to explore the impact that plants have had on life on our planet.

This chapter will help you provide some of these initial experiences for students, but these lessons certainly do not constitute a complete unit on the plant kingdom. In many cases, the lessons can be taught with materials you can gather outdoors, and in others you need to prepare before the lessons by gathering materials from other sources. Sometimes local garden stores, florists, or botanical gardens will donate plant materials to your school science program. In each lesson, students will manipulate some part of a plant or make direct observations, and this will be much more likely to ignite student learning than reading about plants in a textbook.

No matter where you obtain the materials, the experiences your students have with plants are crucial to their understanding of living things. Plants provide the link for humans and all others in the animal kingdom to the greatest source of Earth's energy—the Sun.

If you are not sure where to start with a unit on plants, try bringing a few into your classroom. Simply ask your students to observe the plants and make a list of their observations. Ask students to make a list of questions they have about plants. If you don't have any plants or funds to buy them, try cutting a branch from a tree limb or a shrub and bringing that into the classroom. Even just bringing in a leaf for every student to have at his or her desk would be beneficial as a means to ignite their thoughts about plants' structure and function. These simple ways to introduce plants will get you started, and the lessons in this chapter will allow you to provide experiences that deepen the understanding your students have of how plants fit into the circle of life on Earth.

Resources

Websites

- *www.discoverlife.org*
- *www.fastplants.org*
- *www.plt.org*

Children's Literature

- *The Ink Garden of Brother Theophane* by C. M. Millen (Charlesbridge Publishing, 2010)
- *It's Harvest Time!* by Jean McElroy (Little Simon, 2010)
- *Seeds, Stems, and Stamens: The Ways Plants Fit Into Their World* by Susan Goodman (Millbrook Press, 2001)
- *Ten Seeds* by Ruth Brown (Andersen Press, 2001)

DON'T FORGET!

- Students should thoroughly wash their hands after any visits to the school yard and after handling any materials that have been taken in from outdoors.

- Review students' records for allergies such as those to specific plants or stinging insects.

- When gathering any objects outdoors (rocks, soil, insects, etc.), it is best to look for locations that have not been sprayed with pesticides, herbicides, or other chemicals.

For a full list of safety tips, see page xi.

Objective

Students will understand and demonstrate how water moves through plant material and that water is crucial for the survival of plants.

Topic: Plants
Go to: *www.scilinks.org*
Code: BOS019

Why/How to Use This Lesson

In a unit on plants, it is imperative for students to understand the dependence that plants have on water. Depending on your budget for science lessons, you may want to use plants purchased from a store or plants from your own yard. Some plants generate smaller plants from shoots that take root or seeds that fall to the ground, so you may be able to pull up some small plants to use in this lesson. You'll need several small plants that have their roots attached and can be taken up out of the soil. Consider teaching this lesson at the beginning of the unit so that students have as much time as possible to observe the plants.

Materials

six to eight small plants of the same type, flowerpots or clear plastic containers such as cups with tops, water, student worksheet

Procedures and Tips

1. Before conducting this lesson with students, you should try putting the plants in water yourself. Try two or three different kinds to see which one you want to use in class.

2. Divide your class into groups and give each group a plant to observe. Give each group a plant, preferably planted in soil in a small flowerpot.

3. Have the students gently extract the plant and all roots from the soil, placing it instead

in water. If using cups with tops, students can cut a hole in the top of the cup to make it support the plant.

4. There should be at least one plant left in the soil to serve as a comparison to what happens to the plants in water.

5. Students should observe the plants over at least two weeks.

6. Ask students to make predictions and observations and take notes about what they observe happening to the plants. They can use the chart on the student worksheet and can keep additional notes in a science notebook or journal.

7. Facilitate a class discussion toward the end of the observation period to draw conclusions about how plants use water.

Grade-Level Considerations

For primary grades it would be sufficient to have one plant in soil and one in water in the classroom. You may wish to send seeds home with students to let them try this with parents.

Assessment/Next Steps

Assess student worksheets and science journal entries for reasonable observations about the plants in water. If the plants you have chosen will work outdoors at your school, you could consider planting them in the school yard. Another option would be to put plants back in pots with a couple of different soil types to compare.

Sample Discussion Questions

• What would happen to plants that germinated or were raised without soil? Explain.

• Can plants live without water? Why or why not?

HOW PLANTS USE WATER

Name: _____ Date: _____

Establish a plant in water using materials provided by your teacher. Using a clear container will allow you to see the roots. Make a prediction. What do you think will happen to your plant that is left in water instead of being in soil?

_____

_____

_____

Use the chart below to keep a record of what you see happen with your plant.

Date	Observations of Plant in Water

What did you notice about the plant in water? Did the roots grow? Did the stem or leaves grow?

_____

_____

_____

How could you take this further? What else could you do with the plants?

_____

_____

_____

_____

Objective

Students will compare how plants grow in different soils.

Topic: How Do Plants Respond to Their Environment?

Go to: *www.scilinks.org*

Code: BOS020

Why/How to Use This Lesson

This lesson could be started simultaneously with "How Plants Use Water," since some of the plants in this lesson need to be taken from the soil and placed in a different type of soil.

Materials

clay soil, potting soil, sandy soil, at least three identical plants, trowel or hand spade, water, planting containers, hand lens, student worksheet

Procedures and Tips

1. Give students samples of the three types of soil. Ask them to compare the soils, making close observations using the hand lens. You may also wish to allow them to determine how the soils react to water. They may do so by adding the same amount of water to each type of soil and determining if one is more absorbent.

2. Given three different plants of the same type, students should plant one in each of the three types of soil. Before doing this, students should remove the plants from their original soil and rinse the roots free of the other soil.

3. Students should record predictions of what will happen to each plant and how well each soil will provide what the plant needs.

4. Plants should be measured for baseline data, which can be compared with future growth.

5. Plants can be left in the classroom by a window or a grow lamp and observed over time.

Grade-Level Considerations

For primary grades, reduce the number of soils to two and keep a class chart rather than individual charts.

Assessment/Next Steps

Evaluate student understanding of how each soil might support the needs of the plant. If conducting this lesson along with the "How Plants Use Water" lesson, students can compare growth in water with growth in various soils. If the two are conducted together, then the plants for both lessons need to be the same species. Either way, students can make a graph of the growth of the plants.

Sample Discussion Questions

Do plants grow better in some soils rather than others? Why or why not?

WHAT PLANTS GET FROM DIFFERENT SOILS

Name: _____ Date: _____

Look at the various soil samples you have been given. Use the chart below to organize your observations.

Characteristics	Clay	Sand	Potting Soil
Particle/grain size			
Reaction to water			
Color(s) of soil			

Which soil will produce the best plants? Make a prediction and explain.

_____
_____
_____
_____
_____
_____
_____
_____
_____
_____
_____
_____

Objective

Students will compare two or more different types of leaves, looking for the characteristics of leaves that give them form and function.

Topic: Plant Characteristics

Go to: www.scilinks.org

Code: BOS021

Why/How to Use This Lesson

In a unit on plants, studying leaves gives students a way to relate a familiar object to the science of plants. If you have 30 students in a class, you can have 15 each of two types of leaves, and then students may trade since each student will need two types. This lesson can fit into a study of the parts of a plant or the plant system for distributing water throughout its various parts.

Materials

leaves from two (or more) different species of plants, hand lens, pencils, wax pencils or crayons, student worksheet

Procedures and Tips

1. You may either gather leaves before class or take students into the school yard to choose their own. Either way, students need leaves from two different plants. For this lesson, they need to be flat leaves, not needles from an evergreen. (Safety note: Know the species of plant from which you gather leaves. For instance, use common trees such as oak or maple to avoid plants such as poison ivy and poison oak.)

2. Students should look at the leaves with a hand lens and record details about each leaf.

3. Have students make a leaf rubbing by laying a leaf under the paper in the designated spot and using the crayon or pencil to make the rubbing. They should press down on the leaf and fill in the spot with either crayon or pencil marks. The outline of the leaf should begin to appear in what would otherwise look like a scribble.

4. Ask students to describe to you what they see. Try to steer the conversation toward the lines in the leaf—the veins that carry water into the leaf. The leaf also has a "stem" of its own—the main vein.

5. Discussion can continue to include how a leaf fits into the function of a plant.

Grade-Level Considerations

Not much change is needed to do this lesson with primary grade students, but consider using plain paper for the leaf rubbings instead of the worksheet.

Assessment/Next Steps

Informal assessment of student work may be conducted with a classroom walk-through, viewing work to make sure veins of leaves are showing up in rubbings. Additional leaves may be examined and rubbings made and labeled. More important, discuss with students how the leaf contributes to the function of the plant, and ask questions to verify their understanding. As a follow-up, keeping plants in the classroom allows for additional discussion and observation of how a leaf contributes to the life and daily function of a plant. When you are finished with the leaves, make sure you return them to the outdoors, if possible in a compost bin.

Sample Discussion Questions

- What are the functions of a leaf?
- Why does a leaf wilt?

COMPARING LEAVES

Name: _____ Date: _____

Look at a real leaf that your teacher will provide. If possible use a hand lens to look even closer. What do you notice? Write down at least three observations using complete sentences.

_____
_____
_____
_____
_____

Leaf Rubbings: Use the space below to make leaf rubbings of two different leaves from two different species of plants. Put the leaf under your paper. Rub over the top of it with a crayon or pencil.

Leaf 1	Leaf 2

What is different from one leaf to another? What is the same? Do you see anything that can help water move throughout the leaf?

_____
_____
_____
_____

3

Objective

Students will compare and contrast two or more types of seeds and explore their function.

Topic: Seed Germination

Go to: www.scilinks.org

Code: BOS022

Why/How to Use This Lesson

In a unit on plants, it is important to study seeds and how a plant begins its life. You may be able to get seeds donated from a local hardware store or garden shop. If not, many places sell seed packets for less than a dollar. Depending on how many students you have, two packets of seeds may be enough to teach this lesson. If possible, try to find seeds that have an obvious difference. For instance, a sunflower seed is considerably different from a radish seed.

Materials

two or more different types of seeds, hand lens, rulers, scale (optional), student worksheet

Procedures and Tips

1. Choose two (or more) types of seeds for your students to study. If you have enough seeds, give each student two each of two different types of seeds. You can do this with just one of each if needed.

2. Have students sketch what the seeds look like. If you have enough seeds, you may ask students to tape one of the real seeds onto their paper.

3. Students should also measure the seeds and record the data.

4. If a scale is available, have the students weigh the seeds. They may have to weigh the entire seed package if one seed is not registering

a weight. To calculate the weight of a single seed, divide the weight by the number of seeds in the packet and subtract the weight of the empty packet.

5. Facilitate a class discussion about the function of seeds, what is inside them, and how the two types of seeds your students have are alike or different.

Grade-Level Considerations

With younger students, large seeds such as sunflower, pumpkin, beans, or corn might be easier to handle than small seeds like radish and mustard. Primary grade students can compare seeds, but it may be helpful to keep a class chart instead of individual charts.

Assessment/Next Steps

Assess for reasonable responses on the worksheet chart. From the initial study and comparison of the seeds, the next logical step would be to plant the seeds so that students can watch them germinate. You may want to plant some in soil and allow others to germinate in a clear container with water so that students can see what is above and below what would be the soil surface in a traditional planting. Science vendors and garden stores sell seed germination kits that include containers and rich soil. While these kits are not required, they certainly make it easier to start the seeds and keep the process organized.

Sample Discussion Questions

- What does a seed need in order to grow? What would happen if one of these needs was not met?

- What is inside a seed?

COMPARING SEEDS

Name: _____ Date: _____

Look at the two types of seeds you have. Use the chart below to help you organize information about your seeds.

	Seed 1	Seed 2
Description		
Measurements		
Sketch		

How are your seeds alike or different? _____
_____
_____

What predictions can you make about the plant that would be produced by your seeds? _____
_____
_____
_____

Objective

Students will be able to identify the parts of a flower and how the form of these parts relates to their function.

Topic: Parts of a Plant
Go to: www.scilinks.org
Code: BOS023

Why/How to Use This Lesson

In a unit on plants, learning about flowers helps students understand how a plant can provide for wildlife and at the same time get help in its processes from various insects and other animals.

Materials

flowers; hand lens; dissecting kits or other objects that can serve the purpose such as toothpicks, plastic forks or plastic knives; camera with projector (optional); student worksheet

Procedures and Tips

1. Obtain flowers from a local florist, your garden, the school yard, or a local botanical garden. Many florists will donate flowers for dissection. Many species of lilies lend themselves to dissection because their parts are more obvious than those of some other species.

2. If you have never dissected the type of flower you have for your students, you may want to try dissecting one prior to teaching this lesson. Make sure that you can identify the parts.

3. Before having students dissect flowers, discuss with them the form and function of a flower. What is it designed to do?

4. Students should have some time to look at the flower without the dissection tools.

5. If possible, use a camera with a projector to project a flower that you are dissecting while students are dissecting their own flowers.

Grade-Level Considerations

Students in upper elementary grades or middle school should be able to identify the petals, pollen, stamen, anther, pistil, ovary, sepals, and stigma. Primary grade students can stick to petals and pollen.

Assessment/Next Steps

Circulate during the dissection activity and ask students to identify various parts of the flower. Follow up with a discussion of pollination and seed production at the appropriate level for your students. Observing some living flowering plants in the outdoors would be ideal, but you may also be able to find video of bees or butterflies visiting flowers.

Sample Discussion Questions

- Why do plants have flowers?
- Why are flowers bright colors?

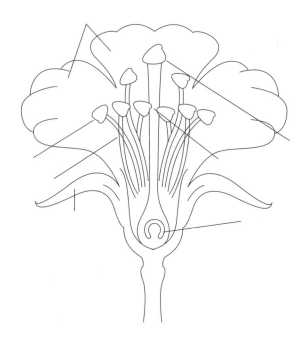

FLOWERING PLANT DISSECTION

Name: _____ **Date:** _____

Name at least one way that a flower helps a plant.
_____
_____

After taking a flower apart, draw a cross section of the flower. Label as many parts as you can.

Moving pollen from flower to flower is helped along by several different creatures. Name as many of those animals as you can. _____
_____
_____
_____

CARNIVOROUS PLANT DISSECTION

Objective

Students will explore the relationship between carnivorous plants and insects.

SCI LINKS.
THE WORLD'S A CLICK AWAY

Topic: How Do Plants Grow?
Go to: www.scilinks.org
Code: BOS024

Why/How to Use This Lesson

In a unit on living things, this activity shows one of the unusual relationships between animals and plants. You may be able to get the dying stalks of pitcher plants from a botanical garden or a local greenhouse. These hollow stalks will contain the exoskeletons of insects that have been eaten by the plant. The plant digests the other parts of the insect, but the hard exoskeleton remains. Revealing these in dissection can help students understand one of the unique relationships between animal and plant. This is the perfect transition lesson from a unit on plants to a unit on insects. (In this book the unit on insects appears first in Chapter 2, but the lessons do not need to be taught in that order.)

Materials

cuttings of pitcher plants and other carnivorous plants; hand lens; toothpicks, plastic forks or knives, or scissors; dissection kits (optional); student worksheet

Procedures and Tips

1. Share some live specimens of carnivorous plants with students if possible; some garden centers and science supply vendors sell them. If it's not possible to obtain live plants, show photographs of them to your students.

2. Divide the class into several small groups and give each group the stalk/pitcher part of a pitcher plant. (As the stalks begin to die, workers at garden centers or botanical gardens may pinch them off and would likely donate them for use in your classroom.)

3. Before giving students any dissection tools, ask them to predict what might be inside the hollow plant stalk.

4. A hand lens will help students look more closely at the remains of insects they will find inside the stalk.

5. Discuss with the class what the plants get from the insects (additional protein) and also how these plants can help control insect populations in moist, swampy areas that have a high concentration of insects.

6. Students can compare the number and types of insects that they and their classmates have found, and graph the results.

Grade-Level Considerations

Students may use dissection kits at the appropriate grade level, or lower grades may use common items such as toothpicks, plastic forks or knives, or scissors to open up the stalk. This lesson may be best suited for upper elementary and middle school students. Very young children may be bothered by the demise of insects in the plants.

Assessment/Next Steps

Check for understanding during a class discussion of the results of the dissection. Ask students to compare and contrast the relationship between insects and carnivorous plants with the relationship between insects (as pollinators) and flowering plants. Consider having a terrarium of carnivorous plants in the classroom for further study.

Sample Discussion Questions

- Is it possible for a plant to "eat" an animal? Explain.

- Why did you find some parts of the insects still in the plant?

CARNIVOROUS PLANT DISSECTION

Name: _____ Date: _____

What do you think is inside the plant stalk?

_____

_____

_____

What did you find?

_____

_____

_____

Make a group graph to show what you found.

Objective

Students will discover and demonstrate how plants are used by humans in at least three different ways during the school day.

Why/How to Use This Lesson

SCI LINKS.
THE WORLD'S A CLICK AWAY

Topic: Medicine from Plants
Go to: www.scilinks.org
Code: BOS025

In a unit on plants, it is important to help students understand the dependence of humans on plants. Ideally, you should have a green plant in the classroom long before you begin the unit on plants, as well as during the unit. Students need to recognize that humans, like other animals, depend on plants as a food source and as a means by which oxygen is recycled. This lesson could even be related to studies that include food chains or food webs in relation to carnivores. While carnivores eat only other animals, some of the animals they consume would be plant eaters.

Materials

various materials that are made from plants such as food items, wooden pencils, plastic water bottles that are also part plant material, an item of cotton clothing; student worksheet

Procedures and Tips

1. Before you begin this lesson, you will benefit from making your own jot list of how you notice that plants are used during the day at school. These could include food items in the cafeteria, plants that serve a decorative purpose indoors or out, and even the cotton that is a component of clothing being worn at school.

2. Ask students to make a jot list of as many uses that humans have of plants as possible. If any of these are encountered during the school day, students may put a check mark beside that item. This activity can be continued near the end of the same day or during the next day, to give students enough time to gather information about how plants are used.

3. Give students the opportunity to meet in a small group with two to four other students in order to compare the uses of plants that each noticed. If students have put check marks beside the uses each one noticed, it would be helpful to put an X or different-color check mark for the uses noticed by others.

4. After students work together, hold a whole-class discussion and ask for examples of what students have noticed about the use of plants. If you notice that there are some areas that students have left out, ask some guiding questions.

5. If possible, use the discussion as a lead-in for the next lesson, "Using Plants to Make Dyes."

Assessment/Next Steps

Assess students on reasonable answers on the worksheet. This lesson can be repeated with a homework assignment over the weekend or a couple of weeknights. If the lesson is started one day and continued the next, you could just include the entire 24 hours in the survey of plant use.

Grade-Level Considerations

Ask primary grade students to come up with just one use of plants in a paired discussion with a classmate. Make a list as a class.

Sample Discussion Questions

- Why do we need plants?
- What would happen if we could not use anything made from a plant for a whole day?

HOW HUMANS USE PLANTS

Name: _____ Date: _____

Make a list of all the uses you can think of for plants.

_____   _____
_____   _____
_____   _____
_____   _____
_____   _____
_____   _____
_____   _____

After going through the school day, put a check mark by all the uses of plants you have noticed. Did you notice any others that were not on your original list?

_____
_____
_____

Work together with other students. What did they notice that you did not? If it's on your list but you didn't check it off, use a different color pen or pencil to check it now.

_____
_____
_____

What was the most common use of plants that you and your classmates noticed?

_____
_____
_____

Was there any use of plants that was noticed by only one person? Were there any that were unexpected? Write a paragraph including these answers and summarizing your experience in looking for the ways people use plants.

_____
_____
_____
_____
_____

Objective

Students will use a plant to produce a color dye.

Topic: How Do Plants
Respond to Their
Environment?

Go to: www.scilinks.org

Code: BOS020

Why/How to Use This Lesson

After the previous lesson on how humans use plants, it will be helpful to explore one human use of plants together as a class. You may consider integrating social studies if your students have standards on Native Americans or Colonial Americans—both groups that frequently used plant dyes. You may also want to bring in a discussion of how heat from the Sun or a hot plate affects plant material.

Materials

plants such as dandelion roots, goldenrod, and berries; white cloth; large jar or gallon jug *or* hot plate and large pot; *The Ink Garden of Brother Theophane* (see the "Resources" section at the beginning of this chapter; optional); student worksheet

Procedures and Tips

1. Discuss historical uses of plants with students. Ask students how pioneers might have used plants of various colors. Try to elicit answers that include using plants to make dyes.

2. Consider reading aloud from the book *The Ink Garden of Brother Theophane,* which tells how color was extracted from plants in the Middle Ages.

3. Students should develop their list of steps individually and then could work in pairs or small groups to compare their steps.

4. You may either buy some berries at the grocery store or take students outside to find plants. Common plants used in dyes can be found by searching the internet; examples include dandelion roots (pink or

red), goldenrod (yellow), black raspberries (purple), and blueberries (light blue).

5. If you choose to make the plant dyes completely inside, use a hot plate to boil the plant parts in water. Once the water comes to a boil, turn the heat down to warm/low and continue to heat until the water is obviously colored. Alternatively, you may wish to describe the process and have the students prepare the plants in school, but then you should boil them after school or at home.

6. Using the Sun to heat the plant parts is a safer way to make dyes and does not require an additional heat source. If using this method, place the plant material in a large jar or jug (gallon) with water and put it in a sunny location for 24–48 hours. Then remove the plant material and put in an article of cloth that can be dyed. The cloth item will need to stay in the jar with exposure to the Sun for one to four days. Consider using a white T-shirt or washcloth. If you want each student to have his or her own item to dye, get donations of large jars from local restaurants and ask each student to bring in a white cloth.

7. Items that have been dyed should not be washed in warm water with other items or the dye can "bleed" to other items.

Grade-Level Considerations

This activity should be done under close supervision or as a demonstration if using a hot plate, particularly for elementary students; you should operate the hot plate when doing this activity with grades K–5. It may be helpful to have the whole class use one plant item, particularly for younger students. You could boil the water ahead of time and have it ready for the students. For upper elementary or middle grades, consider discussing the type of change (chemical or physical) that takes place when making dyes from plants.

Assessment/Next Steps

Assess understanding by checking for reasonable responses on the student worksheet. If you use the Sun dye process, you may suggest to parents that they consider helping students individually at home with the boiling water method.

Sample Discussion Questions

- How did Native Americans or pioneers create dyes before modern conveniences and methods?

- What types of plants or parts of plants have bright colors that could be used to make dyes?

USING PLANTS TO MAKE DYES

Name: _____ Date: _____

Use the chart below to list five specific plants or plant parts that have bright colors.

Plant	Color
Example: Strawberries	Red

Make a list of steps that could be followed to make a dye from plant parts. Add more numbers if you need them.

1.

2.

3.

4.

List the plant item you will use for your dye. _____

What color should it make? _____

After making your dye, write down the results. What happened as expected? What was different than what you expected?

_____
_____
_____
_____

What other uses of plant colors can you think of?

_____
_____
_____
_____

ROCKS AND SOILS

4

Humans have built their homes upon the land, often using the rocks and stones from the land as building materials. Rocks and soil are indeed a part of everyday life and an important component of a complete science curriculum.

Where do teachers get rocks to show students? Often a rock collection is one of the more common materials purchased by schools for science teaching. However, not all schools have rock collections and some cannot afford them. A thrifty science teacher can teach a unit on rocks with only those that can be found in the area. Although some locations may not yield all of the samples that would create a substantial rock collection, there are likely to be enough to share the basic concepts that students need in the elementary and middle grades. The same would be true for soils. Even if there is only one soil type in the area, it can be used as a great starting place for teaching about soils. Local soil can be compared with purchased soil samples (e.g., potting soil or play sand). In fact, it is that comparison that lends itself to great science explorations for young people—comparing both soils and rocks through close observation and hands-on experiences.

Use these resources and the lessons in this chapter to introduce students to rocks and soils in their local area and beyond. Consult your district science curriculum and state science standards to see where these lesson ideas fit best, and consider bringing in a guest speaker from a college geology department, a museum, or a rock and mineral society.

Although these lessons do not constitute an entire unit on rocks and soils, together they do offer an introduction to the important components of the Earth that students see around them every day. Perhaps students will find out why teachers often say, "Science rocks!"

Resources

Websites

- *http://education.usgs.gov*
- *http://www.geosociety.org/educate/LessonPlans/i_rocks.htm*
- *http://school.discoveryeducation.com/schooladventures/soil*

Children's Literature

- *Jump Into Science: Rocks and Minerals* by Steve Tomecek (National Geographic Children's Books, 2010)
- *Rocks, Fossils and Arrowheads (Take Along Guides)* by Laura Evert (Cooper Square Publishing, 2001)
- *Rocks in His Head* by Carol Otis Hurst (Greenwillow Books, 2001)

4

DON'T FORGET!

- Use care when students are asked to use sharp objects (such as those in dissection kits, toothpicks, pipe cleaners, straight pins, rocks, or arrowheads).

- When gathering any objects outdoors (rocks, soil, insects, etc.), it is best to look for locations that have not been sprayed with pesticides, herbicides, or other chemicals.

- When working with water indoors, completely clean up any spills.

For a full list of safety tips, see page xi.

Objective

Students will observe rocks that can be found locally and record their observations.

Topic: Composition of
Rocks

Go to: www.scilinks.org

Code: BOS026

Why/How to Use This Lesson

To develop an understanding of Earth science, students need to start with the basics and in particular something they can hold in their hands. Most children who have spent any time outdoors have picked up a rock at some time, and in this lesson they will not only hold the rock but will take a closer look. This lesson could be used at the beginning of a unit on rocks or as part of a unit on rocks and soils. Consider following this lesson with "Characteristics of Rocks" and "Making a Rock Collection," which cover all three different types of rocks.

Materials

snack-size resealable plastic bags, rocks, hand lens, ruler, scale (optional), student worksheet

Procedures and Tips

1. Show students a rock that you have found nearby. Ask the students to say some words that describe the rock. Tell them that you are going to ask them to bring in their own rock from home. (If this is not possible, provide rocks for them.)

2. Give students a plastic bag to use to store a rock they will collect. Tell them that it must fit in the bag and they must be able to seal it. This will cut down on the size of the rock and prevent unsafe situations that may result from larger rocks being transported on school buses. Place the following note for parents inside the plastic bag:

> PARENTS: Our class is studying ROCKS. Please help your child find a rock from the local area that will fit in this bag. Seal it up and send it to school with your child. Make sure your child knows to keep the rock in the bag until it is delivered safely to my classroom.

3. When students have brought in their rocks, divide the students into groups to compare and contrast their rocks. Ask them to write three sentences describing the rocks on their worksheets.

4. If a scale is available, students may weigh the rocks and determine which is the heaviest. Students may also use a ruler to measure the size of the rock.

5. Determine if all types of rocks (igneous, metamorphic, sedimentary) are represented by the student samples. You may wish to use this lesson to serve as an introduction to the next step—introducing the three types of rocks and their characteristics.

Grade-Level Considerations

Upper elementary and middle grade students may be assigned to research the geological history of the area, using local rocks as a starting point. For primary grade students, attach a note for parents to the plastic bag for the rock collection activity if it is being sent home. Instead of the student worksheet, you could provide a plain piece of paper on which students would draw a picture of their rock, and perhaps a picture of another rock that is different in appearance.

Assessment/Next Steps

Assess student understanding with the sample discussion questions and the responses to the student worksheet. Rocks brought in by students may be organized into a collection that could be

displayed in the classroom or media center. If there are a wide variety of rocks, you may even wish to use a plastic craft box or similar container to make a permanent collection that you would keep in your classroom.

Sample Discussion Questions

- How are any two of the rocks alike? How are they different?
- Describe your rock in terms of weight, color, and texture.

EXPLORING LOCAL ROCKS

Name: _____ Date: _____

Describe your rock in three complete sentences.

_____
_____
_____
_____
_____
_____

Measure your rock and record your data here. Use whatever measuring device is available (for example, ruler or scale). Also compare the rock with a common object (for example, "smaller than a quarter but bigger than a penny" or "weighs about the same as two marbles").

Measurement data: _____

Comparison: _____

Compare your rock with that of another student. Use the chart below to record your observations. Fill in each space with a word that describes one or both of the rocks.

Your Rock	Both	Another Student's Rock

Do you think your rock originally came from the local area or somewhere else? Why?

_____
_____
_____
_____
_____
_____

NATIONAL SCIENCE TEACHERS ASSOCIATION

DON'T FORGET!

- Provide students with a lab safety form or science activity safety form that outlines general science safety procedures. You can use your school system's standard form, if available. If you teach in an elementary school that does not use a standard form, check with a middle school science teacher. The safety form should be sent home to be signed by parents.

- Protective equipment, including but not limited to vinyl gloves, aprons, and eye goggles, is encouraged for the activities in this book.

- When working outdoors, students should be reminded not to look directly into the Sun.

For a full list of safety tips, see page xi.

Objective

Students will explore the characteristics of different kinds of rocks.

Topic: Identifying
Rocks and Minerals
Go to: www.scilinks.org
Code: BOS027

Why/How to Use This Lesson

This activity goes beyond the local geology and guides students in distinguishing the three different kinds of rocks. This understanding is important to developing an accurate concept of the Earth's ever-changing surface.

Materials

samples of igneous, metamorphic, and sedimentary rocks; hand lens; student worksheet

Procedures and Tips

1. For this lesson, you will need to locate samples of the three types of rocks. Most middle schools with adequate science supplies have rock collections, as do some elementary schools. If your school does not, order from a science supply catalog or contact a local rock and mineral society or the geology department of a local college or university to request a loan or donation of rocks.

2. If the rocks are in a kit, try to take enough of them out so that students cannot see any identifying labels.

3. Give the students a set of characteristics of igneous, metamorphic, and sedimentary rocks and then ask the students to classify the rocks they have been given.

4. If your students have brought in their own rocks, ask them to classify those as well.

5. Use the sample discussion questions to generate class discussion.

6. For the last part of the student worksheet (coming up with a creative way to describe a type of rock), assign one of the three types of rocks to your students either individually or in small groups. For instance, if you have six groups of students, then two groups can be assigned igneous, two metamorphic, and two sedimentary. You may wish to write the names of the rocks on small pieces of paper and have them drawn from a bag or basket.

Grade-Level Considerations

Students in primary grades do not need to know the details of the three types of rocks, although this information is appropriate for upper elementary and middle school students. Students in middle grades can go further in depth with some research on differentiation of the formation of the types of rocks.

Assessment/Next Steps

Check the student worksheets to assess understanding. Students should be able to separate a set of rocks into the three categories based on the characteristics of each. As enrichment and extension, consider inviting a local geologist or representative of a rock and mineral society to visit the class and bring some samples of rocks.

Sample Discussion Questions

• What distinguishes each of the three types of rocks?

• How are the rocks from the collection different from (or similar to) local rocks?

CHARACTERISTICS OF ROCKS

Name: _____ Date: _____

Look at the samples of rocks your teacher has provided. Divide them into three categories, and support your choices by recording your observations regarding the appearance of the rocks. Use the chart below to organize your observations. Use the boxes under each category to write words that describe your observations of the rocks.

Category 1	Category 2	Category 3

Now make a chart of the three categories that scientists have used to classify rocks. Use a reference to find words that describe each category.

1.	2.	3.

How did your original list compare with the second list?

_____
_____
_____
_____
_____

Come up with a creative way to describe one of the three types of rocks—for example, a poem, rap, or song.

Objective

Students will collect and classify a variety of rocks.

Topic: Igneous Rock
Go to: *www.scilinks.org*
Code: BOS028

Why/How to Use This Lesson

If students have collected rocks during other lessons in this chapter, use those rocks as a basis for this lesson; or contact a local rock and mineral society or a geologist at a college. Students can benefit from making a rock collection in which rocks are identified by both category and specific rock type.

Materials

rocks from a local source or from a science supply company, containers such as egg cartons or small plastic toolboxes with dividers, computer access (word processing program) or markers to create labels, digital camera (optional), student worksheet

Procedures and Tips

1. Provide students with samples of the various rock types. Students may bring rocks as well, or search for rocks on the school grounds. Students may also bring in egg cartons to use for their collection containers.

2. Give students guidelines indicating the number of rocks you expect in the collection for each category (igneous, sedimentary, metamorphic) and the requirement for identifying the rock by type and specific

name (e.g., obsidian, igneous; or limestone, sedimentary).

3. If students have computer access, they may use a word processing program to create labels for the containers. If not, students may use markers to create labels. Allow students to be creative in labeling and decorating containers for their rock collections.

4. Consider displaying rock collections for a parent night. If the rocks must be returned to school collections or if loaned from other sources, make a record of the student collections with a digital camera.

Grade-Level Considerations

Students in primary grades may be given categories by the teacher such as large, medium, and small. These students may also be asked to classify rocks by color or texture.

Assessment/Next Steps

Student understanding can be assessed by the accuracy with which rocks are labeled. If the rocks and containers used are not assigned as supplies to a certain grade level, you may partner with a teacher in another grade and let the students share the collection and a brief orientation to the rocks with younger students.

Sample Discussion Questions

- How should a rock collection be arranged?
- Why are rock collections helpful to scientists or students?

MAKING A ROCK COLLECTION

Name: _____ **Date:** _____

Make a plan for creating a rock collection. The following guidelines might be helpful. Write your plans for each of these:

Total number of rocks: _____

Number by category: Igneous _____   Metamorphic _____   Sedimentary _____

Type of container you will use: _____

Make a list of the rocks you will put in your collection. If you do not know the names of each one yet, use a descriptor such as "rough, brown" or "flat, smooth."

Igneous	Metamorphic	Sedimentary

Explain how you will further arrange your rock collection. Consider the appearance of the rocks, the possible age of the rocks, alphabetizing them by name, or any other method that you can explain. Your teacher may want to approve the order before you make a final decision, but strong, logical reasoning for your choices will support the idea you have. Think carefully and write down your thoughts.

_____
_____
_____
_____
_____
_____
_____
_____
_____
_____

Objective

Students will research and report how humans have used rocks historically and in the present.

Topic: Rocks and
Human History
Go to: www.scilinks.org
Code: BOS029

Why/How to Use This Lesson

The dependence of humans on natural resources such as rocks helps students understand why it is important to take care of our planet and all that it provides. Consider using this lesson as enrichment during a unit on rocks, or as a science connection in a social studies unit on Native Americans.

Materials

hand lens; arrowheads made from rocks (originals are sometimes available for loan from universities, or reasonably priced [several for $1] replicas can be purchased from vendors); *Rocks, Fossils, and Arrowheads* (see the "Resources" section at the beginning of this chapter); student worksheet

Procedures and Tips

1. Start a class discussion about the ways that humans use rocks. (Possible answers might include in buildings, walls, or fences.) If they do not mention historical uses for hunting or weapons, then ask specifically if any student has ever heard of such a use. Show students an arrowhead.

2. If you have been able to locate replicas of arrowheads, allow students to examine them with a hand lens. (SAFETY NOTE: Some arrowheads can be sharp—check to be sure they are not too sharp for students to handle.)

3. Ask students to consider how the arrowheads were made. You may wish to give students the opportunity to research this using books or the internet. It may be helpful to read aloud to the class a few pages from *Rocks, Fossils, and Arrowheads*.

4. Ask students to sketch the arrowhead they have, and then to sketch how it might have been used historically.

Grade-Level Considerations

Rather than give each student one arrowhead to examine, it would be safer for primary grade students to just look at a sample that you keep in your hands.

Assessment/Next Steps

Check student sketches and descriptions of the use of arrowheads for reasonable responses such as hunting.

Sample Discussion Questions

- What were the first tools used by humans? How were they used?

- How have humans used rocks throughout history?

- How are rocks used by humans in the present day?

HOW HUMANS USE ROCKS

Name: _____ Date: _____

What are some ways that humans have used rocks in historical times?

_____

_____

_____

In the smaller box sketch the historical rock item (or replica) that your teacher has provided, showing details such as shape, markings, and color. Then in the larger box sketch a scene that illustrates the use of the rock item the way it would have been used in the past.

Write a description of the scene that you have created. Use at least three complete sentences.

_____

_____

_____

_____

Objective

Students will compare different types of soils.

Topic: Soil Types
Go to: *www.scilinks.org*
Code: BOS030

Why/How to Use This Lesson

Even though there are great lessons within the local rocks and soils, basic differences between types of soil are important for students to recognize in the overall scheme of Earth science. Use this lesson to anchor other activities where students are looking at soils that have been found outdoors.

Materials

play sand, potting soil, claylike soil sample, plastic containers, hand lens, student worksheet

Procedures and Tips

1. Have one type of soil sample available in a plastic container, and have an extra plastic container. Pour the soil from one container to another and ask students to describe what they see.

2. Give samples of each of the three types of soil to small groups of students. Allow them to touch the samples and examine them with the hand lens.

3. Ask students to record their observations in the chart on the student worksheet.

4. Students should use a textbook, reference book, or the internet to verify the characteristics of soil that they have recorded. Students should compare the three types of soil and make any notes needed to supplement the observations they have written.

Grade-Level Considerations

Think about how to simplify the concept for younger students. It may be helpful to focus on one characteristic of soil such as color. For instance, if you have white sand, red clay, and black potting soil, it may be enough for primary grade students to differentiate the colors.

Assessment/Next Steps

Assess student understanding with the discussion questions below and for reasonable responses on the student worksheet.

Sample Discussion Questions

- Are all soils the same? Why or why not?
- Do all soils react the same way to water or wind? Explain.

CHARACTERISTICS OF SOILS

Name: _____ Date: _____

Write words or phrases in each of the spaces to describe the soils you have examined.

Sand	Potting Soil	Claylike Soil

How were the three types of soil alike?

_____

_____

_____

_____

How were they different?

_____

_____

_____

_____

How do humans use the different types of soil?

_____

_____

_____

_____

Choose one of the three types of soil and list a plant that you think would grow well in it.

_____

_____

_____

_____

Objective

Students will compare and contrast soils from various locations.

Topic: Soil and Climate

Go to: www.scilinks.org

Code: BOS031

Why/How to Use This Lesson

Whether students have lived in one place all of their lives or have moved often, it is likely that they do not think about how soil might be different from one place to another. This lesson will require students to think about the differences in soils from various locations.

Materials

small containers, samples of various types of soil, hand lens, paper plates, student worksheet

Procedures and Tips

1. In your own travels or in those of friends and colleagues, ask for soil samples as a "souvenir" from as many places as you can get them. You might ask a pharmacy for small medicine bottles or find similar-size containers for collecting soil. Small resealable plastic bags will work too. Once you have several soil samples, arrange them in groups so that you have two or three per set that look as different as possible. Label them with letters and make a key that says where they came from (e.g., A = Miami Beach, B = Mount Saint Helens, C = Great Smoky Mountains, Tennessee). Always include a sample of local soil, too.

2. Start your lesson by asking students if soil is the same everywhere. Ask them if they have been anywhere that the soil is noticeably different from the soil around their home. If you live in a strictly urban area, it's possible that students have not seen the natural soil in the area. (Of course this is possible anywhere,

depending on how much experience students have being outdoors both at home and school.)

3. Give two or three soil samples to small groups of students and ask them to fold the student worksheet and then answer the questions on the top half of the worksheet. Give them time to discuss with other group members where they think the soils originated.

4. Give students a key that tells where the soils came from. Ask students to compare the original locations of the soils (as shown on the key) with their predictions and complete the bottom half of their worksheets.

Grade-Level Considerations

For primary grades, simplify by using just two soil samples. Consider using sand and a dark soil. Primary grade students can usually identify that sand is the type of soil on a beach or in the desert.

Assessment/Next Steps

Students should be assessed based on their reasoning regarding where the soil came from, not on accuracy of a specific location where the soil originated. After this lesson, you may wish to ask students to bring back soils from places they visit, perhaps from a grandparent's home or somewhere they visit during school holidays.

Sample Discussion Questions

- Describe the appearance of the soil in the local area.

- Have you ever been anywhere that the soil looked different? Where? Why do you think some soils are different colors from others?

SOILS FROM HERE AND THERE

Name: _____ Date: _____

Fold your paper at the dotted line. Follow your teacher's instructions.
Record your observations of the soils you have.

_____

_____

_____

Make a prediction about their original location.

_____

What evidence makes you choose that location?

_____

_____

(Once all questions above are answered, your teacher will give instructions before you
unfold.)

- FOLD HERE- -

Now you know the actual location where your soils came from. How do the actual
locations differ from your prediction?

_____

_____

_____

_____

_____

Describe the soil that is found in the place you originally predicted. Is the soil there like
the sample you had in any way? Explain.

_____

_____

_____

_____

_____

Objective

Students will identify factors that can cause changes in the surface of the Earth.

Topic: What Is an Earthquake?

Go to: www.scilinks.org

Code: BOS032

Why/How to Use This Lesson

Students may have the misconception that landforms on Earth do not change—or at the very least they may think that landforms do not change often. This lesson will help identify factors that cause or contribute to changes in the Earth's surface features. If you teach a unit on storms or natural disasters, this would be a good lesson to include.

Materials

plastic containers, soil, card stock paper or thin cardboard, scissors, toy cars, toy houses and buildings, twigs, digital camera (optional), student worksheet

Procedures and Tips

1. Discuss the various ways that the Earth's surface can change and how it affects human life (earthquakes, fault lines, volcanoes, erosion).

2. Following the suggestions below, you may wish to make a model that will represent an area that will be hit by an earthquake or a moving fault line.

3. Using a plastic container (shoe box size) for each of several cooperative groups in your classroom, cut card stock or cardboard into pieces that will fit in the container. Bend them once so that they are able to fold and be held down by the soil, yet have a tab or piece that sticks up above the soil. Place them carefully and then fill the container about halfway with soil.

4. Use toy cars or buildings to make a scene of a town or neighborhood. Students can add

twigs to represent trees and use other natural items found in the school yard as they see fit.

5. Once students have their models set up, they can record how it looks with a digital camera or a sketch.

6. Students can pull the tab on the "fault line" and pull it completely out of the container, which should dislodge some of the soil and move the objects that are in the scene.

7. Students should create another sketch or take an "after" photo of the scene.

8. On the worksheet, students should record what they have seen.

9. Another way to do this would be to leave out the cardboard and simply slide the container back and forth vigorously on the tabletop. You may wish to have students measure the distance they slide it each way as a means of comparison among groups. Assign each group a different length (e.g., group 1 will slide it 20 cm each way, group 2 will slide it 30 cm each way, etc.).

Grade-Level Considerations

This lesson would be better as a demonstration for primary grade students. You could have one set of materials in a center that students could later visit in small groups to repeat what you have demonstrated.

Assessment/Next Steps

Assess students on their responses on the student worksheet. You may wish to repeat the process with a larger container, giving students the opportunity to be more creative and test additional setups and hypotheses.

Sample Discussion Questions

What are some of the factors that change land? How do these changes affect what the land looks like?

EARTH'S CHANGING SURFACE

Name: _____ Date: _____

Write a description of a fault line and an earthquake.

_____
_____

Draw a sketch of your model of an area with a fault line.

[ ]

What happened to the scene when you activated the fault line?

_____
_____
_____

Draw an updated sketch that shows what happened after the fault line shift.

[ ]

What changed? How is this like real life?

_____
_____
_____

Objective

Students will study soil erosion caused by water.

Topic: Soil Erosion
Go to: www.scilinks.org
Code: BOS033

Why/How to Use This Lesson

Erosion often changes the surface of the Earth in very visible ways. Students should be able to identify the effects of erosion as one of the many forces that affects the Earth's surface. More than likely, there is erosion somewhere in your school yard or nearby.

Materials

photographs of eroded soil, rectangular plastic containers, soil, water, cup or beaker for water, a variety of household and natural items that can be used to try to control erosion in the student demonstrations, digital camera (optional), student worksheet

Procedures and Tips

1. Show students some photographs of eroded soil. These may be from a book, the internet, or ideally from the school yard or other local area. Ask students to describe what they see.

2. Ask students to watch your demonstration carefully. Using a plastic container with a layer of about 10 cm of soil, tilt it upward at one end and pour water down the center of the soil. Ask students to describe what they see.

3. Divide students into groups of about four students each and give each group a plastic container, at least the size of a shoe box. They should fill it with about the same amount of soil as in the demonstration. All of the containers should be the same size, and the amount of soil in the container should be measured so that it is uniform. Keep one dry container of soil for a control.

4. Ask students to make a plan to slow down the erosion that they saw in your demonstration.

5. Give students a variety of materials with which they may attempt to control erosion in their containers. These may be common household items such as plastic wrap, popsicle sticks/craft sticks, toothpicks, or paper clips; natural items such as small rocks, sticks, or mulch; or any other object that you think would work.

6. After students have an opportunity to create barriers to erosion or preventive measures, each group should pour a consistent amount of water onto the soil with the container tilted up at a uniform level.

7. Pour the same amount of water in the container that only had soil and no preventive measures.

8. Ask students to compare what happened. Based on the amount of soil that stayed in place, find out which group had the most effective erosion control.

Grade-Level Considerations

For primary grades make this a whole-class project with only two containers. Allow students to help decide what to put in to prevent or reduce erosion. Students can draw a picture of what happened and write words or a sentence to describe their drawings.

Assessment/Next Steps

Assess students for reasonable responses on the worksheet. As a next step, consider going outdoors to document soil erosion in the school yard with digital cameras. Students can write about erosion in science journals, and they can compare the same spot a month later to see if it has changed.

Sample Discussion Questions

• Describe what happens to bare soil when there is a large amount of rain.

• Have you ever seen erosion? Describe what you saw.

EROSION

Name: _____ Date: _____

What happened to the soil when the water was poured?

_____

_____

Choose materials to make a barrier to erosion. What will you use? How will you make your barrier? Write your plan in at least three steps.

_____

_____

_____

_____

Make a sketch of your barrier on the left, and then pour the water. Make a sketch on the right that shows what happened after the water was poured.

Your barrier:	Show what happened afterward:

Objective

Students will model the characteristic changing shape of a barrier island and will discover the role of a barrier island in a coastal system.

Why/How to Use This Lesson

Barrier islands are an important ecological and geological part of shorelines. When there is an oil spill or hurricane, it is the barrier island that stands between danger and the mainland. Use this lesson to support standards in Earth science, and consider a further study of barrier island ecology that would address life science standards.

Materials

rectangular plastic containers; play sand; water; plastic representations of trees, buildings, fences, cars, and animals (optional); student worksheet

Procedures and Tips

1. Find an aerial photograph of a barrier island to show students; you can search for barrier island photographs at the U.S. Geological Survey website (*www.usgs.gov*). Ask students what role they think a barrier island plays in the coastal area.

2. Ask students to help you build models of barrier islands and to demonstrate its changing nature. Ask them what materials might be helpful.

3. Add sand and enough water to moisten it to a rectangular plastic container. Have students shape the sand into a model of the mainland shore and a barrier island in front of it. See the figure at the end of this lesson for a top view of the model.

4. Add enough water to model the ocean at the shoreline and to surround the barrier island model. If you are using plastic containers that are about the size of shoe boxes, it works well

to have the "shore" at one of the shorter ends so that the water has plenty of length to move back and forth.

5. The plastic container should then be gently rocked back and forth toward the shore so that water moves back and forth around the barrier island. Compare this to what happens when the tides go in and out twice a day.

6. Students should be able to observe significant changes in the barrier island. They should sketch the changes they see and write about them.

7. Check for understanding with a class discussion.

Grade-Level Considerations

Make this a demonstration lesson for primary grade students rather than having them work in groups.

Assessment/Next Steps

Informal assessment will include teacher observations during the activity and reasonable responses on the student worksheet. If you have given students relatively small containers for group work, the next step might be using a much bigger container for a larger model. If you live in a coastal area, consider a field trip to visit barrier islands, or invite a scientist who has researched barrier islands in your area. Coastal geologists would be a good resource, as would information from organizations such as the National Oceanic and Atmospheric Administration (NOAA; *www.seagrant.noaa.gov*) and Centers for Ocean Sciences Education Excellence (COSEE; *www.cosee.net*).

Sample Discussion Questions

- What is the meaning of the word *barrier*?
- What do you think we can demonstrate with this barrier island model?
- How do barrier islands change over time?

BARRIER ISLANDS

This is a representation of what the barrier island models should look like from above:

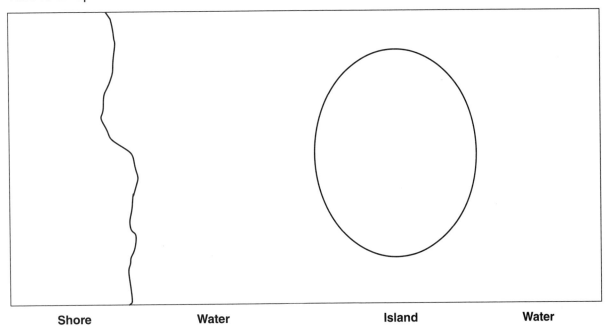

Shore   **Water**   **Island**   **Water**

BARRIER ISLANDS

Name: _____ Date: _____

Write a definition of a barrier island in your own words.

_____

_____

_____

Draw a sketch of your model of a barrier island.

What happened to the island when you moved the water to simulate waves?

_____

_____

After moving the water back and forth at least 10 times, draw an updated sketch.

What changed? How is this like real life?

_____

_____

_____

NATIONAL SCIENCE TEACHERS ASSOCIATION

WATER

5

ater is the key to life on Earth. It is part of the unique combination of factors that makes our planet the best suited for supporting plant and animal life. It is what space exploration often seeks to find on faraway planets. Whether it's frozen or tropical, water is home to unique life forms. No wonder living things find a home in Earth's water. It makes up three-fourths of the surface of the Earth.

Not only is water a source that sustains plant and animal life, it is also a source of energy when its power is harnessed. It provides a means of transportation for plants and animals, and humans have made use of the world's waterways, oceans, and lakes with a wide array of vessels ranging from rafts and canoes to incredibly large ocean liners that move people and goods from one landmass to another. Because it is so important to those who inhabit the Earth, students need to explore the role of water. Where does water go when it flows down a river? Can water move land? What is the most effective way to use water to grow plants? These are just a few of the questions that students can explore with the lessons in this chapter.

These lessons may all be part of a thematic unit on water if accompanied by additional learning activities. Project Wet training (*www.projectwet. org*) gives educators credible and thorough water education credentials and encourages community involvement in water quality projects.

WATER

No matter how "deep" the curriculum on water studies, this topic is important for all people on Earth. Knowing how to harness water's power, keep it clean, understand its flow, and respect its power will help all students develop the level of understanding needed to sustain and even improve the quality of water in their communities.

Resources

Websites

- *www.education.noaa.gov*
- *www.projectwet.org*
- *http://water.epa.gov/learn*
- *http://water.usgs.gov/education.html*

Children's Literature

The Water Cycle by Bobbie Kalman and Rebecca Sjonger (Crabtree Publishing, 2006)

DON'T FORGET!

- When gathering any objects outdoors (rocks, soil, insects, etc.), it is best to look for locations that have not been sprayed with pesticides, herbicides, or other chemicals.
- When working with water indoors, completely clean up any spills.
- When working outdoors, students should be reminded not to look directly into the Sun.

For a full list of safety tips, see page xi.

Objectives

Students will model the water cycle and make observations of the water cycle in action. Students will learn the terms *condensation, evaporation,* and *precipitation.*

SCI LINKS
THE WORLD'S A CLICK AWAY
Topic: Water Cycle
Go to: www.scilinks.org
Code: BOS034

Why/How to Use This Lesson

It is important for students to understand the finite amount of water on the Earth's surface and to see a closed water system in action.

Materials

gallon plastic bags, fine-point permanent marker(s), sand, water, straws, student worksheet

Procedures and Tips

1. Students should be given the opportunity to find a resource (textbook, reference book, or internet) for information on the water cycle and make a diagrammed sketch of the cycle on the student worksheet or on plain white paper. Plain white paper may be best, but the worksheet is provided as a guide. Check to make sure the elements of the water cycle are all present (including condensation, evaporation, and precipitation).

2. Students should slip the paper into the plastic bag and then use a fine-point permanent marker to trace the water cycle on one side of the bag.

3. Have the students remove the paper from the plastic bag and put enough sand in the bottom of the bag to make it stand up.

4. Have the students add enough water to the bag to moisten the sand.

5. After leaving enough space to put a straw in and blow air to fill the bag, students should seal the bag.

6. Put the bags close to a classroom window so the sunlight shines on them. Students should be able to see condensation form on the inside of the bag and then precipitation should fall down into the sand, and the water cycle will start again with evaporation.

Grade-Level Considerations

For primary grades it is not necessary to include the terms *condensation* and *precipitation*; instead just make references to clouds that form and rain that falls. Primary grade students can learn the word *evaporation*; even if some students cannot spell it accurately, they can say the word and understand its meaning in a simple way. Students at this level can make their own water cycle bag, but they may need additional support from an adult helper such as a paraprofessional or a parent volunteer.

Assessment/Next Steps

Assess students on successful completion of making the water cycle in a bag and for proper use of the terms *condensation, evaporation,* and *precipitation.*

Sample Discussion Questions

• When a mud puddle dries, where does the water go?
• How can it rain over and over and not flood the entire Earth?
• How does your model of the water cycle work?

EARTH'S WATER CYCLE

Name: _____ Date: _____

On this page, draw the remaining parts of the water cycle. Use arrows to show the movement of the water. Use these words as labels: *condensation, evaporation,* and *precipitation.* You can add any other words you find helpful.

POLYMERS—HELPING SOIL HOLD WATER

Objective

Students will explore polymers that are used to hold water in potting soil.

Topic: Soil Erosion
Go to: www.scilinks.org
Code: BOS033

Why/How to Use This Lesson

While it seems logical that outdoor science would feature mostly life or Earth science, it is important to consider physical science connections that support and integrate with the other fields.

Materials

pair of clear containers (e.g., jars, drinking glasses, beakers), other clear containers (e.g., small beverage cups), polymer (from Educational Innovations or other vendor), water, potting soil samples (one water retaining, one not; optional), student worksheet

Procedures and Tips

1. Start with a discrepant event. Using the pair of clear containers, fill one with water and the other with the polymer and water so that the polymer is "invisible" to students. Have this set up ahead of time so that students do not see what is in each container.

2. Ask students to observe the two containers carefully and to share their observations with the class. (Questioning may be helpful: How are they alike? What is in them? How are they different? Is the same thing inside each?)

3. Discuss what the students have observed. Show the students the polymer without water, in its round, dry form. Ask students what uses there might be for a product like this. Introduce the idea of potting soil or garden soil that helps to hold water for plants. If possible, allow students to examine an example of such a soil product.

4. Use a measured amount of water and soil to test if it works well for holding water. You will need some potting soil that is plain and not designed to hold water.

5. Put the two types of soil in separate clear containers such as small beverage cups. Students should put the water in and then touch the soil to see how it feels. They should also make observations from the side of the clear cup.

6. Observe the cups an hour later and a day later to see if there is any change. You may wish to place the cups in the sun by a window or even outdoors.

Grade-Level Considerations

This lesson is best for upper elementary and middle grades, and could be used as a demonstration of polymers for primary grades. Two sizes of the polymer are available; use the larger size for primary grades.

Assessment/Next Steps

Assess students for reasonable responses on the student worksheet. To take this lesson further, consider planting some flowers or vegetables in two pots, one with the water-holding soil and one with plain potting soil. Students can record their observations on both the soil's moisture and plant growth.

Sample Discussion Questions

- Describe the appearance of the water. Did it look like it had anything in it?

- How could people benefit from using this type of polymer?

- How does the soil appear and feel after this much time has passed?

106

NATIONAL SCIENCE TEACHERS ASSOCIATION

POLYMERS—HELPING SOIL HOLD WATER

Name: _____ Date: _____

Can you think of ways to help soil that is used to grow plants hold water?

_____

_____

_____

What have you observed in a flowerpot or a place outdoors where there are plants?

_____

_____

_____

How do you think the material your teacher has given you can help soil hold water?

_____

_____

_____

Compare soil with this material and soil without. What is the difference? Write your observations in sentence form and make a line or bar graph to show the evidence in the box below.

_____

_____

_____

Objective

Students will model energy that comes from water and compare and contrast two or more models.

Topic: Water Properties
Go to: www.scilinks.org
Code: BOS035

Why/How to Use This Lesson

Many students have never seen a dam yet they benefit from water supplies harnessed by dams or electric energy that is generated from the controlled release of water from a dam. This lesson allows students to model early attempts to capture water power by making a waterwheel. It can be a connection to social studies standards on early American history or using natural resources to produce energy.

Materials

photographs of waterwheels, plastic containers of various heights and sizes, pitcher or bucket, balsa wood or Styrofoam plates or trays, popsicle sticks, plastic spoons, toothpicks, hot glue/ glue gun, water, brick (optional), water pump (optional), student worksheet

Procedures and Tips

1. Using the internet or reference books, find pictures of waterwheels from factories, mills, or in historical photographs.

2. Ask students to work in pairs using the materials given to design and build a waterwheel.

3. The waterwheel can be powered by pouring water into a plastic container from a pitcher or bucket. If the container is rectangular, the waterwheel can rest in the middle and the container can be tilted up by resting one end on a couple of books or a brick. This will make the water flow.

4. Alternatively, a water pump that is sold commercially for decorative ponds or larger aquariums could pump water in a manner that would move a water wheel.

5. Allow students to demonstrate their waterwheels for the class, asking other students to make observations about how each waterwheel works.

Grade-Level Considerations

For primary grades make this a class project rather than having students work in pairs. The teacher can put the waterwheel together for the class while letting the students select materials with some guidance.

Assessment/Next Steps

Use the student worksheet as an assessment tool to determine student understanding. If possible, make a field trip to a historical mill or a place that has a waterwheel. Consider an interdisciplinary connection to social studies standards.

Sample Discussion Questions

- How can water help produce power?
- Which materials produced the most effective waterwheel model?

USING WATER TO HARNESS ENERGY

5

Name: _____ Date: _____

What is the energy source for a waterwheel? How does it work?

_____

_____

_____

What materials will you use to model a waterwheel? Make a list and draw a sketch of your waterwheel.

_____

_____

Use books or the internet to conduct some research. What uses did waterwheels have in American history?

_____

_____

_____

What modern uses are there for energy harnessed from water? What future uses would you predict for water as an energy source?

_____

_____

_____

_____

Objective

Students will compare and contrast salt water and freshwater.

Topic: Freshwater
Ecosystems

Go to: www.scilinks.org

Code: BOS036

Why/How to Use This Lesson

Bodies of water—including oceans, lakes, rivers, and creeks—are found throughout and surrounding the continent. Students can benefit from exploring which ones are salt water and which are freshwater, as well as physically touching both types of water. Use this lesson to tie science and social studies standards together.

Materials

clear plastic cups or beakers, water, iodized table salt, hand lens, microscope (optional), student worksheet

Procedures and Tips

1. Prepare by filling one clear cup with tap water or bottled water and another clear cup with 1 part iodized table salt to 10 parts water. Do this for each group of three to five students and have each group examine the two cups of water. Do not give students the worksheet until after they have had time to determine the difference in the two water samples. Ask them to determine how the two water samples are different; do not tell them up front that one is freshwater and one is salt water. Students should use a hand lens, and when possible a microscope, to look closely at the samples. During the process students may smell the salt and come to a conclusion based on their sense of smell. They may notice a slight difference visually, with the salt water appearing slightly cloudy

or having a whiter appearance than the freshwater.

2. After examining the two types of water and recording their observations, students should research the percentage of the Earth that is covered in water and the amount of that water that is salt water versus freshwater.

3. Ask students to create graphs in the space provided on the student worksheet.

4. Using the sample discusssion questions to spark students' thinking, hold a class discussion to check for understanding.

Grade-Level Considerations

For primary grades, use a globe to show students the amount of water on Earth rather than have them conduct research. Consider reading a book about oceans or other bodies of water to supplement their knowledge.

Assessment/Next Steps

Assess for reasonable answers on the student worksheet and accurate representation of the Earth's water on student graphs. For next steps, ask students to create a multimedia presentation on local bodies of water, or divide the class into groups and assign an ocean or sea to each group. Have them plan and present creative poems, skits, raps, or dances that depict the body of water they have been assigned.

Sample Discussion Questions

- How do oceans, rivers, or lakes affect our everyday lives?

- Have you ever been swimming in the ocean? How is it the same as or different from a swimming pool?

FRESHWATER VERSUS SALT WATER

Name: _____ Date: _____

How much of the Earth's surface is water? Use one of the circles to draw and label one side of the globe, and use the other to make a pie chart that shows the amount of water versus land on Earth.

What did you notice when you looked at samples of salt water and freshwater? How were they alike? How were they different? Fill in the Venn diagram to answer these questions.

Use this space to make a bar graph that shows the percentage of water in oceans, rivers, and lakes. If you want to include a category for "other" you can, or specify ponds, creeks, canals, glaciers, etc.

Objective

Students will compare and contrast macroinvertebrates with larger animals that live in water.

Topic: Aquatic
Ecosystems

Go to: www.scilinks.org

Code: BOS037

Why/How to Use This Lesson

Students in elementary school are typically familiar with aquatic animals like fish and turtles, but often they are not as familiar with macroinvertebrates.

Materials

microscope, pond or creek water, small containers, water dropper, student worksheet

Procedures and Tips

1. Give students the worksheet and ask them to write down the name of an animal that lives in the water. It doesn't matter if it is freshwater or salt water. If the students are in upper elementary or middle grades, make sure they are more specific than "fish" or "turtle"—look for responses such as "trout" or "snapping turtle."

2. Ask students if they believe that we can see all animals. Some students may answer that some animals have to be seen with a microscope or hand lens, and that is the perfect time to tell them that today's lesson will feature animals that must be viewed under a microscope.

3. You may wish to prepare slides ahead of time, or have students use a dropper to put a drop of water on a microscope slide.

4. Allow students to look at the water drops and identify small animals (macroinvertebrates) that are swimming in the drop.

5. Ask students to compare the macroinvertebrates with the animal that they named earlier using the chart on the worksheet. Students may also sketch the macroinvertebrates that they have seen.

Grade-Level Considerations

For primary grades use a microscope that connects to a computer for projection on a screen to show students the macroinvertebrates. They can just be called small water animals for students in kindergarten or first grade.

Assessment/Next Steps

Look for reasonable responses on the comparison chart on the student page. To take this activity further, find a guide to macroinvertebrates (a good online resource is *http://water.epa.gov/learn*) and have students identify the specific species they have seen in water samples.

Sample Discussion Questions

- Are all living things easily visible to humans? Explain your answer.

- How are small water animals (macroinvertebrates) like larger animals that we can easily see?

- What surprised you about the macroinvertebrates that you observed?

ANIMALS THAT LIVE IN WATER

Name: _____ Date: _____

Name an animal that lives in water. _____

Do you think that all living things can be seen by humans? Why or why not?

_____

_____

_____

Follow instructions to fill in this chart:

Put the name of the water animal you listed here: _____	_____

MEASURING WATER FOR A DAY

Objective

Students will keep records of the amount of water that they use in one full day.

Topic: Water
Conservation
Go to: www.scilinks.org
Code: BOS038

Why/How to Use This Lesson

Having a fresh supply of water is some-thing that is often taken for granted. Track-ing the amount of water that is used in a day can help students identify ways that they may conserve water. (See also the "Saving Water" lesson in Chapter 1.) It also gives them the opportunity to practice measurement.

Materials

student worksheet, pencil or pen, calculator

Procedures and Tips

1. Hold a class discussion about how much water students think that they use during a day. Ask students to write down a prediction about their water use on the student worksheet.

2. During the school day, students should put a check mark next to the appropriate activity on the worksheet each time they use water (e.g., drink from water fountain, wash hands).

3. Students should be instructed to continue this record keeping throughout the evening and bring in the results the next day. If you choose, you may make this a school-day project so that you have more control over getting results from every student.

4. Have students compare their predictions with the results. Consider adding everyone's numbers together as a class.

Grade-Level Considerations

This can easily become a class project for primary grades to do during the school day.

Assessment/Next Steps

Assess students on accuracy in comparing pre-dictions with actual water use and for reasonable answers to questions on the student worksheet. To extend this lesson, students may visit a lower-grade classroom and explain what they did to keep track of water usage. Students could develop a list of activities involving water use and ask other students in the school to keep track. Con-sider inviting a guest speaker from the local water utility company. Representatives of these com-panies often give away water-saving devices for showers that reduce water flow. You can contact the company to request that the representative bring enough of these devices to be distributed to the parents of all the students.

Sample Discussion Questions

- How much water do you think you use in one day from the time you get up until you go to sleep?
- Which of your daily activities do you think require the most water? Why?
- Explain how you could use less water in a day.
- How does water conservation benefit your community?

MEASURING WATER FOR A DAY

Name: _____ Date: _____

Predict the amount of water you use during one day from the time you wake up until the time you go to sleep.

_____

Here are some activities that require water. Add others and keep track of them for the day. Put a check mark beside the activity each time you do this.

   Brushing teeth:

   Flushing toilet:

   Others:

Add up the amount of water you used for a day. Compare it with your prediction. Write three sentences that compare your prediction with your results, and what may have surprised you about the results.

_____

_____

_____

_____

List two ways you could reduce your water usage in a normal day.

_____

_____

_____

_____

Objective

Students will model drought conditions and identify problems that are caused by droughts.

Topic: Water
Conservation

Go to: www.scilinks.org

Code: BOS038

Why/How to Use This Lesson

When rainfall amounts in an area are not sufficient to keep drinking water flowing and plants in good health, a drought takes place and causes a multitude of challenges for humans. Use this lesson to help students understand some of those problems and challenges, and to help students recognize the importance of conserving water even at times when there is no drought.

Materials

plants and/or seeds, soil, two identical flowerpots or other planting containers, water, student worksheet

Procedures and Tips

1. Have two identical flowerpots or other planting containers and two plants that are as close to identical as possible. You may also use seeds, but a plant would be the best for illustrating the effects of a drought in a short time. Note that this is not a one-day activity. You will need to water one plant every day, and not water the other plant. Depending on the other factors (room temperature, amount of sunlight, etc.), the plant with no water should begin to wilt within a few days or about a week depending on the type of plant. You should experiment with the plants before you try this with your class to determine about how long it will take for the plant to wilt.

2. Students should have their worksheets available through the duration of the experiment over several days in order to record their observations.

3. Once there is an obvious difference in the two plants (e.g., wilted or discolored leaves), have the students record final observations.

4. Wrap up the activity with a class discussion. Students may share if their predictions were accurate or how they were different from what took place.

Grade-Level Considerations

This lesson can work well for primary grade students because there are only two flowerpots to be handled by students. The worksheet can be simplified or replaced by having students draw pictures of their predictions as opposed to writing sentences.

Assessment/Next Steps

Assess students on reasonable predictions that are supported with sound statements based on prior experience. Consider having students research drought-resistant plants and planting a "drought garden" at the school. Students could also look for water-saving measures such as rain barrels.

Sample Discussion Questions

- Explain what happens when there is no rain for several days or weeks.

- How long can a plant survive without water? Explain.

- What is the first indication that a plant needs water? Why does this happen?

DROUGHTS

Name: _____ Date: _____

Write down the steps you and your class are taking to study how a drought affects plants.

_____

_____

_____

_____

_____

_____

What is the first sign of a drought you will notice?

_____

How many days will it be before you notice this sign? _____

What has happened after…?

One day: _____

Two days: _____

Three days: _____

Five days: _____

Seven days: _____

After you have finished making observations, compare your prediction with what happened. What, if any, were the differences in your predictions versus what actually happened?

_____

_____

_____

_____

_____

_____

_____

5

Objective

Students will determine the percentage of a fruit's weight that is water.

Why/How to Use This Lesson

Students can understand that there is water content in food when they bite into a juicy apple or orange or watch a parent cut open a watermelon. However, most students probably do not realize that some fruits and vegetables have water as the largest part of their contents. This lesson will help students collect evidence regarding the amount of water in a common type of fruit.

Materials

fruit (e.g., apple, banana, orange, or pear), scale, knife, bowl, access to a microwave (or regular oven and cookie sheet), student worksheet

Procedures and Tips

1. Start your lesson by asking students to look at an apple or other piece of fruit. Ask them what is inside of the fruit. If a student answers that water (or juice) is a part of what is inside the piece of fruit, get a prediction as to how much of the fruit is water by percentage or fraction.

2. After taking several answers, use a scale to weigh the fruit and ask students to record the weight. If working in groups, students can record the weight of the particular piece of fruit the group has.

3. Ask students to discuss how you might remove the water from the fruit.

4. Using the internet (either before class as the teacher or in class for students), research methods used to dry fruit in a microwave or conventional oven.

5. The fruit will need to be sliced. (SAFETY NOTE: Slicing the fruit should be done by an adult. Ask the school cafeteria for help with this. Because of weapons policies, be sure to check with an administrator before bringing a sharp knife into the classroom.)

6. If you choose to use a microwave oven, try to bring one into the classroom so that students can observe the process. If using a conventional oven, try to get the cafeteria manager at your school to help you so that the fruit can remain in the school. (If the prospect of getting help at the school to do this is too much, you can take the fruit home with you and dry it in your home oven or microwave.)

7. Students will need to weigh the dried fruit again to compare with the original weight. Put all slices of the dried fruit in a bowl and weigh it on the scale. Subtract the weight of the bowl from the total to get the actual weight of the dried fruit.

8. Students can use math skills to find the difference in the weight and calculate that difference as a percentage of the original weight.

Grade-Level Considerations

With younger students, instead of having them work in groups just dry one piece of fruit for the whole class to observe. Students should rely on visual observation of the fruit before and after drying to see the difference. The scale can also be used if available.

Assessment/Next Steps

Assess students informally based on their participation, as well as for reasonable responses on the student worksheet. As a follow-up, consider bringing in a food expert such as a nutritionist or chef to discuss the water content in common food items. Students may also research animals that get all of their water needs from fruits or vegetables. If you want to demonstrate this, you can have living mealworms in the classroom that get all of their water needs this way. They like potatoes and need oats for solid food as well.

Sample Discussion Questions

- Do we only get the water our body needs from drinking liquids? Explain.

- How much water do you think is in a piece of fruit such as a _____? (Fill in the blank based on what fruit you will be using in class.)

IS THERE WATER IN FRUIT?

Name: _____ Date: _____

Type of fruit or vegetable: _____

Predict the weight of a fruit that your teacher provides: _____

What percentage of that weight is water? _____

With your teacher, explore ways to remove water content from fruits or vegetables. Why would one want to do this?

_____

_____

_____

_____

After the process you have used, weigh the fruit again and record the weight: _____

Find the difference between this weight and the original weight. Use this number to determine what percentage of the piece of fruit is water:

_____

Are you surprised at the percentage? Explain.

_____

_____

_____

_____

_____

_____

_____

IN THE SKY 6

Whether it is a good science activity or not, it may be difficult to find a child in many schools that has not "modeled" clouds by pasting cotton balls on construction paper. It may also be difficult to find a seasoned science teacher who would disagree that it would be better to observe real clouds in the sky by simply walking in the school yard or looking out a classroom window. The natural curiosity of a child often draws their eyes toward the sky, and there is no reason why educators should not take advantage of students' inclination to gaze upward.

Whether students are looking at objects in space or within the Earth's atmosphere, there are abundant resources to support teaching about the sky and beyond. Agencies such as NASA and the National Oceanic and Atmospheric Administration (NOAA) have a large online presence with lesson ideas and background information that can be helpful to teachers at all grade levels. Children's literature also addresses many related topics in effective ways that can be incorporated into interdisciplinary instruction anchored by science concepts.

The lessons in this chapter touch on the major topics that can be addressed on this subject, but they only represent a small portion of what can be accomplished through engaging students in thoughtful observations of both the day and night skies. The sky is literally the limit.

6

Resources

Websites

- *www.education.nasa.gov*
- *www.education.noaa.gov*
- *www.epa.gov/enviroed*
- *www.globe.gov*
- *www.theweatherchannelkids.com*

Children's Literature

- *Come See the Earth Turn: The Story of Léon Foucault* by Lori Mortensen (Tricycle Press, 2010)
- *Erased by a Tornado!* by Jessica Rudolph (Bearport Publishing, 2010)
- *Follow the Drinking Gourd* by Jeanette Winter (Knopf Books for Young Readers, 2008)
- *Global Warming* by Seymour Simon (Collins, 2010)
- *Life on Earth—And Beyond: An Astrobiologist's Quest* by Pamela S. Turner (Charlesbridge Publishing, 2008)
- *Look to the Stars* by Buzz Aldrin (Putnam Juvenile, 2009)

DON'T FORGET!

- Provide students with a lab safety form or science activity safety form that outlines general science safety procedures. You can use your school system's standard form, if available. If you teach in an elementary school that does not use a standard form, check with a middle school science teacher. The safety form should be sent home to be signed by parents.

- When working outdoors, students should be reminded not to look directly into the Sun.

For a full list of safety tips, see page xi.

Objective

Students will collect evidence (photographs or sketches) and write descriptions of clouds in the sky.

Why/How to Use This Lesson

Topic: Clouds
Go to: www.scilinks.org
Code: BOS039

Sometimes in everyday life, we need to be aware of the weather conditions that surround us. Students can learn to make predictions about precipitation based on clouds they see in the sky, and this knowledge will benefit them throughout their lives.

Materials

digital camera(s) or sketch paper and pencils, student worksheet

Procedures and Tips

1. Follow local weather forecasts and observe the sky to choose a day that has clouds for students to observe.

2. Provide opportunities for students to observe clouds throughout the course of the day using either digital cameras or sketch paper and pencils. These observations could be made from the classroom window, during outdoor recess or physical education, or as a homework assignment on the way out of the school building. Just make sure students make the observations all on the same day.

3. Ask students to describe what they saw. Elicit descriptive answers beyond "clouds in the sky"; look for detail such as "long skinny clouds" or "dark puffy clouds." Ask students to make predictions about what precipitation, if any, might result from the clouds.

4. Find a local weather forecast on the internet or record a forecast from television and show one of these to your class. Compare what happened after students observed clouds with their predictions and those of the internet or television forecast.

5. Discuss the results and help students understand that forecasts are predictions (a hypothesis) based on evidence.

Grade-Level Considerations

For kindergarten and first-grade students, it is enough that they recognize that clouds appear in the sky before it rains, and sometimes when it doesn't rain. They do not need to know about different types of clouds. Depending on state standards, students in second and third grades may be expected to begin to differentiate among the appearance of various clouds.

Assessment/Next Steps

Assess students' responses on the student worksheet, including how thoroughly they describe the clouds they have seen. Consider inviting a meteorologist from a local television station to come speak to your class about clouds and precipitation.

Sample Discussion Questions

- Do all clouds look the same? Why or why not?
- Describe the information can we get from looking at clouds.

CLOUDS AND PRECIPITATION

Name: _____ Date: _____

What do the clouds you see look like? Write descriptive sentences or phrases that give details about what you see.

_____
_____
_____
_____

What do you think might happen as a result of these clouds? If you predict precipitation such as rain, be specific regarding the rain such as "heavy rain lasting for at least two hours" or "rain sprinkles all day tomorrow."

_____
_____
_____

Find a forecast on television or the internet for your area. How does it compare with your prediction?

_____
_____
_____

The next day:
What actually happened?

_____
_____
_____

Are weather forecasts always accurate? Why or why not?

_____
_____
_____

What other evidence can be used to predict rain, sleet, snow, or other precipitation?

_____
_____
_____

Objective

Students will collect evidence of the Sun's impact on objects on Earth.

Topic: The Sun
Go to: *www.scilinks.org*
Code: BOS040

Why/How to Use This Lesson

The Sun's energy provides the Earth with heat and light. In this lesson, students will examine how the Sun's heat impacts objects on Earth. This has practical applications in daily life such as choosing materials or colors for clothing based on weather conditions (e.g., wearing dark colors on cold days). As students continue to build on their knowledge of how various materials respond to heat and light, it will help them understand other related concepts such as insulators versus conductors.

Materials

thermometers, containers in which the temperature will change as a result of being in sunlight, various colored sealable containers or sealable containers made of various materials, student worksheet

Procedures and Tips

1. Follow local weather forecasts and observe the sky to choose a day that is sunny for this activity.

2. Ask students to brainstorm how you might gather evidence of the Sun's heat on the Earth. It is likely that they will mention a thermometer.

3. Unless you have a classroom window that gets a great deal of sunlight, this activity will require putting some objects outdoors and then collecting them later in the day. Ask students to choose three different containers from several that they think will have different inside temperatures when placed in the sun. The containers could be

common items that are found in many homes such as an empty paint can, a plastic food storage container, a small plastic toolbox, an envelope, a cardboard box, an old purse, or any container that can be closed. Try to use containers of three different colors and three different materials in order to get various temperature readings.

4. Place a thermometer in each of the containers to take outside, and have a thermometer to measure the outdoor temperature outside of the containers.

5. After a given amount of time (at least 30 minutes) students should collect the containers and immediately look at the temperature upon opening the containers. You can do this as a whole class with just three containers, or you can have several sets of three containers and do this as group work.

6. Students should record the temperatures on their worksheet and draw conclusions about which colors or materials absorb heat more readily.

Grade-Level Considerations

For the primary grades this should not be group work. You might consider making a simple worksheet with pictures of the three containers. Ask students to circle the one they think will be the warmest after sitting in sunshine.

Assessment/Next Steps

Assess students on their reasoning behind their predictions. To take this lesson further, older students would be able to plan a second experiment using different containers. As enrichment, you might consider ordering beads that change color as a reaction to the ultraviolet light from the Sun.

Sample Discussion Questions

- Explain the benefits that the Sun provides for Earth.

- Have you ever worn clothes made of black cloth on a very hot day? What would happen if you did?

THE SUN AND ITS IMPACT ON EARTH

Name: _____ Date: _____

List three ways that the Sun helps life on Earth.

_____

_____

_____

With your class or group, choose three different containers to place in the Sun with a thermometer inside. Make a numbered list predicting which will be the warmest after 30 minutes or more in the sunshine.

Container (in Order of Prediction)	Prediction for Inside Temperature	Actual Temperature After Being in Sunshine
1.		
2.		
3.		

How were the results of your experiment different from what you expected?

_____

_____

_____

_____

Why are people advised to wear dark colors in cold weather or light colors in warm weather?

_____

_____

_____

_____

DON'T FORGET!

- Students should thoroughly wash their hands after any visits to the school yard and after handling any materials that have been taken in from outdoors.

- When gathering any objects outdoors (rocks, soil, insects, etc.), it is best to look for locations that have not been sprayed with pesticides, herbicides, or other chemicals.

For a full list of safety tips, see page xi.

Objective

Students will explore the benefits of using stars for navigation.

Topic: The Stars and
Keeping Time

Go to: www.scilinks.org

Code: BOS041

Why/How to Use This Lesson

This lesson can be used to integrate science and social studies. It can relate to units on early world explorers who traveled by ship to discover new worlds or to a unit on the Civil War using the book *Follow the Drinking Gourd*.

Materials

Follow the Drinking Gourd (see the "Resources" section at the beginning of this chapter), balls to represent stars (can be various sizes), telescope (optional), gourd cut open to show students the literal meaning of drinking gourd (optional), student worksheet

Procedures and Tips

1. Discuss with students the objects that are in the night sky and how humans have used stars for navigation at various times. Consider reading aloud from *Follow the Drinking Gourd* (the Big Dipper constellation was known to slaves in the Civil War era as the Drinking Gourd).

2. Have students use balls to represent the stars. The balls don't have to be the same size. (Students can search the internet for information on the stars in the Big Dipper.)

3. Have students use science textbooks or a resource on the internet (e.g., *www.nasa.gov*) to determine the distance between each of the stars in the Big Dipper.

4. Once the distance has been determined, students can figure out a scale model using a small unit, such as centimeters or millimeters, to represent each larger unit of measure.

5. Ask the students to hold the balls up and stand in the shape of the constellation with the scaled distance between them.

6. You can either divide your class into groups of seven and have each group model the Big Dipper or choose other constellations and divide the class accordingly. If each group models a different constellation, they can show it to their classmates and expose them to a wider variety of star formations.

7. Ask students to draw a representation of the Big Dipper and at least one other constellation.

8. Ask the class to reflect on the models of the constellations and what it would have been like for stars to be the tool used for navigation. Students should record their thoughts about this on their worksheet.

Grade-Level Considerations

Do not use the student worksheet for primary grade students. Limit the discussion of objects in the night sky to general references to the Moon and the collective group of stars in the sky.

Assessment/Next Steps

Assess students on active participation in modeling the constellations and reasonable responses to the prompts on their worksheet. As a follow-up consider having a telescope available at a school event that takes place in the evening, or hosting a portable planetarium in your school (see *www.e-planetarium.com* and *www.starlab.com* for information on portable planetariums).

Sample Discussion Questions

• Have you ever noticed patterns of stars in the night sky? Describe what you have seen.

• What are some modern ways that people navigate or find their way?

6

Name: _____ Date: _____

Draw a sketch of the Big Dipper.

Draw a sketch of another constellation.

What would it have been like to try to escape slavery with only the stars to guide you? Write a paragraph in response to *Follow the Drinking Gourd*.

_____

_____

_____

_____

_____

_____

_____

Objective

Students will explore Earth's place in the solar system and when possible view planets in the night sky.

Topic: Studying Earth
From Space
Go to: www.scilinks.org
Code: BOS042

Why/How to Use This Lesson

When students look at the night sky, they will usually see stars and sometimes a couple of the planets in our solar system if they know what they are looking for. Help students understand the movement of planets in the solar system by giving them the opportunity to model the system.

Materials

models of the planets and the Sun (inflatable, plastic, Styrofoam, or paper cutouts), student worksheet

Procedures and Tips

1. Before you teach the lesson, search the internet for a reputable site that gives scale models based on a certain size Earth or Sun. Choose a model or representation of the planets. The model can be store-bought or made from construction paper.

2. Divide students into groups of nine—one for the Sun and one each for the eight planets. Give each student the model of a planet or the Sun and ask them to "order" themselves in the correct lineup.

3. Though the classroom will not have enough space for students to model the distance to scale of the solar system, they can model the movement of the planets as described in steps 4 and 5.

4. First have students walk around the Sun (revolve). Ask them if this is the only movement that the planets make. The hope is that students will think about the fact that the Earth revolves on its axis as do other planets. Try to elicit this answer.

5. Then have students "revolve" and "rotate."

6. Discuss with students whether or not their model is to scale. Students may wish to conduct internet research to determine the distance between their "planets" or models if they were modeled to scale.

Grade-Level Considerations

For primary grades, do not use all of the planets. Consider just the Sun and the Earth, or the Earth and its Moon.

Assessment/Next Steps

Informal assessment will include students' ability to work together to model the movements of planets in the solar system. Check for reasonable responses to prompts on the student worksheet.

Sample Discussion Questions

- Explain the movement of the planets in our solar system.

- How much space would we need to create a scale model of the solar system if the Sun model is approximately 30 cm in diameter?

OUR SOLAR SYSTEM

Name: _____ Date: _____

Work together with students in a group to model the solar system and the movements of the planets. Fill in the chart for your model:

Student	Holding Model of	Diameter of Planet Model
	Mercury	
	Venus	
	Earth	
	Mars	
	Jupiter	
	Saturn	
	Uranus	
	Neptune	
	The Sun	**Diameter of Sun Model**

What movement(s) did you or others modeling planets have to make? How does this represent what happens in the solar system?

_____
_____
_____
_____

Do some internet research to find out how much space you would need to create a scale model of the solar system using the diameter of your planet models.

_____
_____
_____
_____

FLYING ANIMALS

Objective

Students will observe and identify the characteristics and adaptations of flying animals such as birds, insects, and bats.

Topic: Adaptations of Animals

Go to: www.scilinks.org

Code: BOS043

Why/How to Use This Lesson

The ability to fly is an adaptation that not only helps animals travel but also helps them to survive. This lesson might be part of a unit on living things and their adaptations, or it can be paired with other activities in this chapter for a unit on objects in the sky.

Materials

feathers; insect wings; binoculars to watch the sky outdoors *or* streaming video of flying animals; hand lens; photographs (from books or the internet) of birds, insects, and bats; projector (optional); student worksheet

Procedures and Tips

1. Provide an opportunity for students to view birds and flying insects either outdoors or using the internet. Bats will likely have to be viewed by streaming video (e.g., from National Geographic or YouTube).

2. Collect feathers and/or insect wings that have fallen to the ground outdoors. Allow students to handle the feathers and wings and to examine them with a hand lens.

3. Find photographs of the three types of animals online and project them on a screen in the classroom, or provide books with photographs of the animals for your students.

4. Ask students to compare the animals in a classroom discussion and to take notes on the chart on the student worksheet. Ask students to choose one of the three animals and write about what would happen to the animal if it could not fly.

Grade-Level Considerations

For primary grades, choose just two of the animals (birds and bats make a good pairing) and have a class discussion on how they are alike and how they are different.

Assessment/Next Steps

Assess students on their answers on the worksheet and their ability to distinguish the benefits of the ability to fly. To follow up, consider asking students to make their own video of flying animals.

Sample Discussion Questions

- What advantages does flying give to animals like birds or bats?

- What would happen if these animals could not fly?

FLYING ANIMALS

Name: _____ Date: _____

Use this chart to take notes about birds, bats, and flying insects.

Birds	Bats	Flying Insects

Choose one of the three animals. Fill in the blank, finish the sentence, and write two more sentences about this.

If a _____ lost the ability to fly, then … _____

_____

_____

_____

_____

_____

Objective

Students will gather evidence of air pollution in the school or in the school yard.

SC*i*LINKS.
THE WORLD'S A CLICK AWAY

Topic: Air Pollution
Go to: *www.scilinks.org*
Code: BOS044

Why/How to Use This Lesson

Though air looks "clean" to students, they may be surprised to learn what particulates are present.

Materials

Clear tape (such as wide packing tape), scissors, index cards, string, hand lens, student worksheet

Procedures and Tips

1. Students will use tape and an index card to make a device that will show evidence of air pollution or particulates.

2. Instruct students to fold the index card in half and cut out a rectangle shape. Cover the hole that was created with wide, clear packing tape. Punch a hole at one end and tie a piece of string on it to hang it up. Help students find places to hang them. If possible, hang some outside the classroom window and some in the classroom. You may be able to find additional places in the school to hang them.

3. Allow students to make visual checks of the "pollution catchers" until there are visible particulates on the tape. This may take a week or more, or it may happen rather quickly.

4. Take the devices down and allow students to examine what is on the tape with a hand lens. (SAFETY NOTE: Check student records for dust allergies to avoid any problems.)

5. Ask students to record their observations on the student worksheet, and discuss the observations as a class.

Grade-Level Considerations

For primary grades the teacher can make the pollution-gathering card or have parent volunteers help students with this.

Assessment/Next Steps

Assess students for reasonable responses on the worksheet and for participation in class discussion and following directions to create their pollution catcher. To take this lesson further, send instructions home and ask students to make the same device to place in the home or outside a window of the home. Students can compare the results at home with those at school.

Sample Discussion Questions

What does the tape look like before it is placed out to collect "pollution"? How will it look after another day? How will it look after three more days?

AIR POLLUTION

Name: _____ Date: _____

Make a prediction about the evidence of pollution you will gather with the card/tape device. What do you think will happen?

_____

_____

After one day:

_____

After three days:

_____

After five days:

_____

After posting your pollution card in the school or outside, look at it carefully with a hand lens. Make a sketch of your observations.

What do you see? Write a description. How is it like or different from your expectations?

_____

_____

_____

_____

Objective

Students will model the usefulness of wind to nature and humans.

Topic: Wind Currents
Go to: www.scilinks.org
Code: BOS045

Why/How to Use This Lesson

Wind is something that all students are familiar with, but it's probably not something they have spent much time thinking about. The wind is an important force in shaping the Earth's surface and is part of many different types of weather events. Use this lesson to help students understand how scientists measure the wind.

Materials

paper cups, construction paper, straws, straight pins, pencils, hole punch, electric fan, bags, student worksheet

Procedures and Tips

1. Engage students in a discussion of times when they have experienced a windy day. Ask if they have ever flown a kite or watched something blow in the wind. Ask students how they know the wind is blowing by looking through a window to the outdoors.

2. Students may choose between making a pinwheel or an anemometer. (See sketches on p. 139.) If possible you should make one of each ahead of time so that students can see what each looks like.

3. Students should make their device and answer the prompts on the student worksheet.

4. Use an electric fan in the classroom so that students can test their devices. If possible, also allow students to test their devices outdoors. If this is not possible, supply plastic grocery bags or something similar to transport the pinwheels and anemometers so that students can take them home.

5. Students may follow up with research on harnessing wind power using modern windmills.

Grade-Level Considerations

For primary grades, parent volunteers could help students make a pinwheel. The anemometer should be saved for upper elementary and middle grades.

Assessment/Next Steps

Assess students on following directions and participation, as well as on reasonable responses to the student page prompts. To take this further, consider pairing this lesson with others that are related to weather conditions. Check out the website *www.globe.gov* to learn how students can report weather data to a worldwide project. For enrichment, you might consider painting a compass rose around the school flagpole. If the wind is strong enough to move the flag, it should point to the compass direction in which the wind is blowing.

Sample Discussion Questions

- How do we know the wind is blowing if we are inside?

- What are some observations we can make when the wind is blowing?

Assembling a Pinwheel or an Anemometer

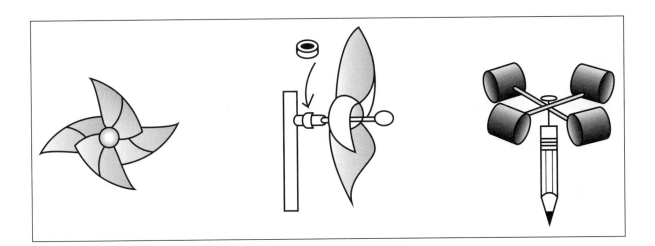

HOW DOES WIND HELP US?

Name: _____ Date: _____

What signs of the blowing wind can you see by looking out a window?

_____

_____

_____

Why is it important for meteorologists to warn people when they forecast extreme wind conditions?

_____

_____

_____

I am making _____ an anemometer or _____ a pinwheel.

How is the device like a windmill that actually can be used to capture wind energy?

_____

_____

_____

Try out your device using the fan provided by your teacher. Make a simple drawing of what happened using arrows to show the direction of the air.

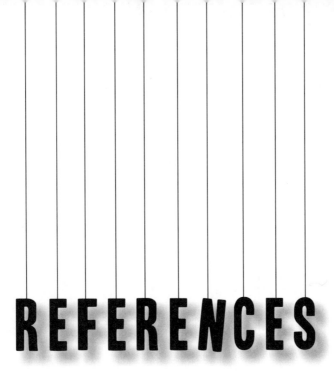

REFERENCES

Ansberry, K., and E. Morgan. 2010. *Picture-perfect science lessons, expanded 2nd edition: Using children's books to guide inquiry, 3–6*. Arlington, VA: NSTA Press.

National Research Council (NRC). 1996. *National science education standards*. Washington, DC: National Academies Press.

National Research Council (NRC). 2011. *A framework for K–12 science education: Practices, crosscutting concepts, and core ideas*. Washington, DC, National Academies Press.

Rich, S. 2005. *Outdoor science classroom: Easy lessons and learning spaces*. Greensboro, NC: Carson-Dellosa Publishing.

Rich, S. 2010. *Outdoor science: A practical guide*. Arlington, VA: NSTA Press.

ANSWER KEY

Chapter 1: Greening the School

Recycling School Paper

- For estimating amount of paper used, accept reasonable numbers based on your judgment. Stop after adding all the totals together to get the daily total for the whole class. The daily average used by one person in the class should be determined by adding together all of the totals for each student and then dividing by the number of students in the class. The average for a typical student in the school can be determined by adding the averages for all classes and then dividing by the number of classes. To determine the average for multiple classrooms (e.g., all classes on your grade level), add the averages for all the classrooms and then divide by the number of classrooms.

- Ways to reduce paper might include writing on the front and back of a piece of paper, erasing instead of starting over with a new piece of paper when a mistake is made, and asking permission to e-mail homework when possible.

- Students can use the estimate of 17 trees to make one ton of paper to determine the number of trees needed for a year of paper at your school.

Going Paperless

- Acceptable responses to the question about electronic tools include whiteboard, laptop computer, projector, and remote answer devices; there may be other reasonable suggestions.

- For the teacher survey, assist the students in delivering this survey to your colleagues; the totals should add up to the number of teachers surveyed.

- Student plans for going paperless will vary, but they should include multiple electronic means of delivering information (e-mail, whiteboards, computers, projectors, etc.).

Composting Cafeteria Waste

- Composting returns natural materials to the Earth and reduces waste in landfills. Benefits of a compost bin include creating rich soil supplements for gardens and reducing garbage.

- Descriptions of the compost bin will vary based on what you provide for students to observe, but biodegradable items such as fruit peels and coffee grounds should be included.

- All other responses to the worksheet depend on individual classroom and teacher circumstances. The question about rate of decomposition will likely get answers stating that the process is slow.

Using Solar Energy

- For temperature locations, encourage students to choose diverse places such as by a window, by a door, in the center of the room, and perhaps beside a desktop computer that gets warm.

- The data gathered and the responses will depend on the temperatures in your classroom. You might want to try this experiment before doing it with the class to see what temperatures you record; you

ANSWER KEY

will then be able to compare your students' results with your results to make sure the students' results are within a reasonable range.

- For the question asking for conclusions, students should recognize that various factors affect indoor temperature and give examples to support their conclusions.

Saving Electricity

- The jot list may include items such as computer, clock, electric pencil sharpener, light fixtures, and projector.

- Examples of electricity wasted at school and corresponding suggestions for energy savings may include doors being propped open, with the suggestion of keeping doors closed so air conditioning or heating doesn't escape; and lights left on in the classroom while at lunch, with the suggestion of turning off lights when leaving the room.

- Examples of electricity wasted at home and corresponding suggestions for energy savings may include leaving a computer on all day, with the suggestion of turning it off when not in use; and leaving lights on when away from home, with the suggestion of using a timer to turn lights on at dusk.

- For the first question on alternative energy, one possible response is wind energy. The wind turns blades on giant windmills, and this energy turns a large turbine that produces electricity, which can be used in homes and businesses. For the second question on alternative energy, solar energy for home or school is a good response. Many homes and public buildings use solar energy effectively, and homes can be retrofitted with solar panels long after the home is built.

Saving Water

- For the table on water use at school, the water fountain may be given as an example. An estimate of 5 gallons/day is reasonable, and a reasonable suggestion to save water is to limit each student's time at the fountain.

- Responses to the question on ways that people have tried to reduce the use of water may include rain barrels to collect outdoor water for flower beds and devices that slow the amount of water coming out of showers.

Reuse!

- Check that the materials selected are logical and practical for each game part.
- You may accept a variety of answers for game title and number of players.
- Check to see if the instructions/rules are step by step and easy to follow.

Helping Teachers Recycle More

- The jot list should include a variety of paper and plastic items.
- The graph responses depend on student choices, but check for reasonable numerical data.

ANSWER KEY

- The total amount of recyclable material should be expressed as either number of items or weight.
- Students should subtract to find the difference in number of items (e.g., number of soda cans recycled by two classes) or weight of the recyclables. For the latter, a student could first weight him- or herself on a bathroom scale and then stand on the scale with a bag of recyclables; to determine the weight of the recyclables, the weight of the student should be subtracted from the weight while holding the bag.
- To determine how much of the recyclable material could be gathered, students should multiply the total by 4 (weeks) to get the total for one month and then by 9 (months) to get the total for the school year.

Encouraging Recycling at Home

- The jot list should include various common items such as aluminum cans, plastic bottles, and glass.
- For an item to track, students may name a commonly recycled item such as newspaper or aluminum cans.
- Numerical data on the weekly chart will vary from student to student, but look for reasonable responses. Similarly, check for reasonable answers to the question on weight.
- To determine how much trash could be kept out of landfills by recycling, the weight of the item should be multiplied by 4 weeks for a month of recycling and by 52 weeks for a year of recycling.
- For the data comparison, numerical answers will vary but students should use addition and subtraction to get answers.

Community Cleanup Project

Responses to the writing prompt will vary, but students should include reference to litter and write the number of sentences assigned.

Chapter 2: Insects

Bug Zoo

- The jot list should include appropriate words to describe the insect that was observed (e.g., small, long-legged).
- A possible response to the question on how a scientist would use this list to classify insects is that the description helps the insect be grouped with similar insects or differentiated from others.
- In comparing insects, students should list words that are opposite or inconsistent.
- The sketch should be an appropriate representation of insects that were observed.

Observing Insect Behavior

- For the behavior observations, students may choose a behavior such as eating or hopping; look for reasonable responses such as "I expect to see the insect hop at least 10 times."

ANSWER KEY

- The nature of the graph will depend on the observations, but check for reasonable responses.
- For the questions on the meaning of the graph and conclusions, student responses will vary but should correspond to information in graph (e.g., "The insect did not hop as many times as I expected. Perhaps they only use this behavior when threatened.")

Insect Food Chain

- The Sun is the energy source for the food chain.
- The plant box should include a plant that insects eat, such as milkweed.
- For Insect 1, students should sketch an insect that eats plants (e.g., a cricket).
- For Insect 2, students should sketch a predator insect (e.g., praying mantis) that eats the prey insect shown in the Insect 1 box.
- An appropriate response to the question about a prey insect's defense is that it can hop away in one big leap (if the insect is a cricket).
- An appropriate response to the question about difference from natural habitat is that crickets may blend in better.

Predators of Insects

- The answer to the question of which animal is the predator depends on what you provide (e.g., spider, praying mantis).
- For the question about predator reaction, possible answers include aggressive action toward the prey insect, chasing the insect, hiding, and moving faster to get away.
- Possible predator advantages include being larger, being faster, and having strong jaws; possible predator disadvantages include being easily visible, especially if the prey has great eyesight.
- An advantage to humans of these predatory relationships is that insect predators help control the insect population in a natural way without chemicals.
- Other types of animals that are predators of insects include bats, birds, frogs, snakes, small mammals, and turtles.
- Acceptable answers for the jot list of living things in a food web include plants and animals such as bats, birds, and snakes.
- The food web sketches will vary, but check for viable relationships in the web.

What's the Difference Between a Spider, an Earthworm, and an Insect?

- Various answers are acceptable on the traits chart; differences may be noted in number of legs versus no legs, type of skeleton, eyes, etc.
- Sketches will vary, but if there are legs make sure there are eight for spiders, six for insects, and zero for earthworms.

NATIONAL SCIENCE TEACHERS ASSOCIATION

ANSWER KEY

- Various answers are acceptable for the three most distinguishing features of the animal sketched (e.g., spiders have eight legs and the ability to spin a web).

Fly, Hop, or Walk?

- For the chart of insects that move in different ways, acceptable answers include the following examples: walking—roach and caterpillar; hopping—grasshopper and cricket; flying—bee and butterfly.
- The following are possible responses to the questions on differences in legs: nonfliers sometimes have "pro-legs" that are smaller; sometimes walkers have longer legs.
- It's beneficial to have insects that move/travel in different ways because insects provide a food source in different parts of the ecosystem. Flying insects like mosquitoes, flies, and bees might be food sources for bats or birds. Insects also "clean up" decaying organic matter, so decomposition depends heavily on insects. Insects such as ants, praying mantises, and caterpillars that walk instead of flying would be potential food sources on the forest floor. How animals travel determines where they can go—and gets them there to devour decaying animals and plants.
- For the question on why flying/hopping insects also need to be able to walk, various answers are acceptable. Sample answers: "Being able to walk could help an insect with an injured wing survive." Bees fly through the air but need to walk inside a hive."
- Responses to the "super" insect question may be in the form of a sketch or a verbal description; either one may include large legs, large wings, or additional eyes or legs. Advantages would include the ability to escape predators.

How Insects Help Humans

- There may be various answers to the question on evidence of the original state of the organic material (e.g., a potato that weighs 35 grams).
- Predictions will vary but may include changes in weight or size.
- An example of an acceptable response to the question of what would change if insects were added is that insects would eat part of the potato, resulting in much lower weight.
- Entries on the chart will vary, but check for reasonable responses.
- For "Notes and Observations," a variety of responses that document the process are acceptable.

Plants as a Habitat for Insects

- The answers to the first two questions will vary depending on the type of plant observed. Examples of insects that call the plant home may include caterpillars and aphids.
- Entries on the chart will vary (e.g., chewing and crawling may be listed as insect activities; plant observations may include bite marks on a leaf).
- The plant helps the insect by providing food and shelter.

ANSWER KEY

- The insect helps the plant by controlling plant population, stimulating new growth (by biting off the leaf or the stem), or preying on other insects that are more harmful to the plant.

Insect Metamorphosis

- Among other acceptable responses for the chart, advantages of metamorphosis include the ability to survive in various places and the fact that the offspring do not compete with the parent for food; disadvantages include vulnerability in the dormant stage and the fact that the insect sometimes must travel to go through phases (one stage in water, one on land).
- The sketch should include either three or four stages of metamorphosis, depending on the insect.

Pollination Nation

- Entries on the data chart will vary depending on the type of opportunity provided to see pollination in action.
- An acceptable response to the question on how scientists could use similar data is that they could repeat experiments, possibly getting different results, to study insect populations and their responses to environmental changes.
- Pollination is important in nature because it is essential to plant reproduction. If no pollination took place for a year, fewer plants would be present in the next growing season.

Wearing a Skeleton on the Outside

- Entries on the chart will vary, but examples of acceptable answers include "structure" for both exoskeleton and endoskeleton and "protection" for exoskeleton.
- An insect with no skeleton would lack structure and be more vulnerable to prey.
- A human with no skeleton would have no structure to make the typical human form and would not be able to move as humans normally do.
- The sketches of the exoskeleton model and descriptive sentences will vary, but check that students understand how the model is similar to and different from a real exoskeleton.

Chapter 3: Plants

How Plants Use Water

- For the prediction, various answers are acceptable but might include "the plant will die" or "the plant's roots will grow fast without soil in the way."
- The observations chart should have a succession of dates over a week or more. Various observations are acceptable but might include "No changes yet"; "Roots are growing"; or "New leaves are starting to appear."
- Responses to the question about what students noticed can be taken from the chart and additional thoughts of students.

ANSWER KEY

- Examples of acceptable responses regarding how to take this further would be to try growing the same plants in both water and soil and to try growing the same plants in water from two different sources, such as indoor tap water and a pond.

What Plants Get From Different Soils

- Possible responses for the observation chart are filled in below:

Characteristics	Clay	Sand	Potting Soil
Particle/grain size	Small, clumping	Large, separate	Variable, moist
Reaction to water	Absorbent	Water sifts through	Looks muddy
Color	Reddish brown	Light brown to white	Black, dark brown

- For the question about which soil will produce the best plants, examples of acceptable answers are "potting soil because it is packaged or produced for growing plants" or "clay because it holds water well." Sand could also be correct, depending on the plant (a cactus or palm tree can thrive in sand).

Comparing Leaves

- Various detailed sentences should be included in the leaf observations.
- Leaf rubbings will vary depending on what leaves you provide, but ideally they should show the lines of the leaf and the overall shape.
- In response to the final questions, students should note that even if the shape of two leaves is different, they both have a main part that connects them to the plant stem, and there are visible veins to move water.

Comparing Seeds

- The descriptions, measurements, and sketches on the seed charts will vary depending on the seeds provided, but check for accuracy.
- Seeds should be compared and contrasted in terms of their appearance.
- Students may make predictions about the plant that would be produced by the seeds based on prior knowledge about the seed or based on the appearance of the seed.

Flowering Plant Dissection

- Acceptable responses to how a flower helps a plant vary but include "attracting pollinators" and "producing seeds."

- Check the cross-sectional drawing for accuracy in labeling the parts of the flower.

- The list of pollinators may include but is not limited to hummingbirds, bats, butterflies, and bees.

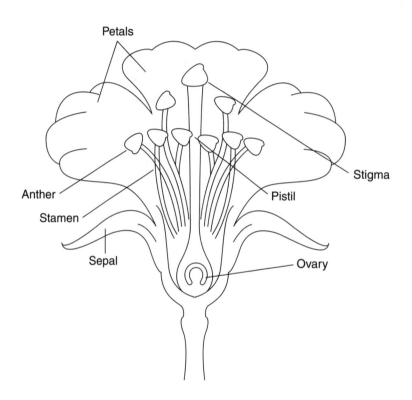

Carnivorous Plant Dissection

- For the question about what is inside the plant stalk, accept reasonable predictions and guide students toward insects as a possibility.

- Students should find exoskeletons of insects that are common to the area.

- The graph should probably be a bar graph with numbers of each item or type of insect (e.g., 18 insect legs, 6 exoskeletons of crickets).

How Humans Use Plants

- For the list of plant uses, acceptable responses include but are not limited to erosion control, decorating homes or yards, and food such as salads and fruits.

ANSWER KEY

- The check marks (or different-color marks) in the follow-up lists will depend on the answers to the first question.
- There will be various answers to the most common use of plants, but food and landscaping are likely and acceptable responses.

Using Plants To Make Dyes

- Possible plant and color entries for the chart include indigo plant, blue; red rose petals, pink; yellow lilies, yellow; and blueberries, light blue.
- The following is a possible answer to the list of steps to make a dye from plant parts: (1) Pick flowers or other parts of the plant needed and mash them up with a mortar and pestle or other tool. (2) Soak them in water for several hours or overnight (one-third plant parts to two-thirds water). (3) Add a cloth item to the mixture to add color (white fabric will work best), and leave it for at least two hours. Longer time in the mixture may make the color darker.
- Students may expect darker colors than they get.
- Other uses of plant colors may include ink and cosmetics (makeup).

Chapter 4: Rocks and Soils

Exploring Local Rocks

- Accept rock descriptions that provide details such as "My rock feels rough on all sides and is gray and black" or "The speckled white and beige rock is smooth with rounded edges."
- Measurement data will vary depending on the rock.
- Sample answers for the comparison chart are filled in below:

Your Rock	Both	Another Student's Rock
Smooth all over	At least partially smooth	Smooth on one side
Colors include black, gray, white	white	Colors include white, beige, light orange

- For origin of the rock, accept a variety of answers as long as the student supports his or her ideas.

ANSWER KEY

Characteristics of Rocks

- Sample answers for the two charts are filled in below:

Category 1	Category 2	Category 3
Brown	Gray	Black
Rough	Smooth	Jagged
Jagged	Rounded edges	Shiny

1. Igneous	2. Metamorphic	3. Sedimentary
Sometimes jagged	Rough	Layered
Darkly colored	Made up of several rocks	Pressed

- For the comparison of the two lists, possible answers include "They were completely different" or "There were some words that were the same but not all."
- Use your discretion to evaluate students' use of related vocabulary in a poem, rap, or song.

Making a Rock Collection

- Plans for creating a rock collection will vary, but check that students fill in all the categories (e.g., total number of rocks is 15, with 5 each of igneous, metamorphic, and sedimentary; type of container is a craft box).
- For the chart, accept a variety of answers as long as they are in the correct categories.
- In response to the question about further arranging their rock collection, students may add size, color, texture, or other categories.

How Humans Use Rocks

- For the first question, students may say that rocks have been used as tools or building materials.
- The rock sketch should be a simple but accurate representation of the rock (or replica) you have provided.
- The scene sketch should depict appropriate use of the rock or stone tool.
- The description of the scene will depend on the sketch; one example might be Native Americans using bows and arrows with arrowheads made of stones or rocks. Check that at least three sentences are used to describe the scene.

152

ANSWER KEY

Characteristics of Soils

- Sample answers for the chart are filled in below:

Sand	Potting soil	Claylike Soil
White	Black	Brown
Beige	Mushy	Thick
Grainy	White specks	Tiny grains

- Sample answers to the question of how the soils were alike: "Sand and clay were both grainy" and "Potting soil and clay were both dark in color."

- Sample answers to the question of how the soils were different: "Grain size was different in clay and sand" and "Sand was white and soil was almost black."

- For the question of how humans use the different types of soil, sample answers include using sand for playgrounds or around swimming areas on lakes or rivers, using potting soil for planting, and using clay for molding pots or for building.

- Possible answers to what plant would grow well in a certain type of soil include cactus in sand and coneflower in potting soil.

Soils From Here and There

- Acceptable observations of soils would include color, texture, grain size, etc.

- Predictions about the original location of the soils will vary; any prediction is acceptable.

- In response to the question of evidence for a predicted location, accept any valid reasoning (e.g., "I think it's from a desert in Arizona because I have seen pictures that show orange rocks and soils in the desert.").

- In response to the question of how the actual location differs from the prediction, accept any reasonable answer (e.g., "I thought it was from Arizona because it was orange, but it's actually from Georgia, where there is some red clay that looks orange.")

- To describe the soil in the predicted location, students should use a book or the internet to research soils.

- Sample answer to the question of whether the soil in the predicted location is like the sample the student had: "Yes. The orange soil from Georgia is probably from the northern part of the state where they call it 'red Georgia clay.'"

Earth's Changing Surface

- Sample acceptable description of a fault line and an earthquake: "A fault line is where the crust of the Earth's surface has separated, where tectonic plates slide past one another and a line or crack

appears in the surface of the Earth. An earthquake is a sudden movement of the ground when there is significant movement, such as when tectonic plates slide past one another or after a tsunami hits."

- The first sketch of an area with a fault line should show an uneven line across part of the Earth's surface.

- In response to the question of what happened to the scene when they activated the fault line, students should say that there would be large-scale movement of rocks and the Earth's surface on either side of the fault line.

- The updated sketch should show damage to buildings after the fault line shift.

- In response to the question of what changed in the model and how this is like real life, students may answer that there is damage to buildings or shifts in hills and mountains, and that the same things happen in real life.

Erosion

- In response to the question of what happened to the soil when the water was poured, a sample answer is "The soil moved and a small 'ditch' was created."

- A sample plan for making a barrier to erosion might include the following steps: (1) Break some craft sticks in half, and use a couple that are whole. (2) Build a little wall half a craft stick tall with the whole ones to support it. (3) Hold it together with metal clips.

- Sketches will vary but should include a visible erosion barrier.

Barrier Islands

- Sample of an acceptable definition of a barrier island: "A barrier island is near the coast of a larger land mass and protects it from hurricanes and extreme ocean tides and conditions. It is home to a wide variety of plant and animal life."

- Sketches will vary but should show an island, water, and mainland.

- When asked what happened to the island when they moved the water to simulate waves, students should respond that the island changed shape, moved, or got smaller.

- The second sketch should show change, including the overall shape or size of the island. Barrier islands change frequently in real life.

Chapter 5: Water

Earth's Water Cycle

Sketches should show condensation, precipitation, and evaporation (with these three words as labels), with arrows going from groundwater to clouds and then back down again.

ANSWER KEY

Polymers—Helping Soil Hold Water

- Accept a variety of answers regarding ways to to help soil that is used to grow plants hold water. Sample answers: "Use a planting pot that has no drain hole in the bottom" and "Mix clay with potting soil."
- Sample observation in a flowerpot or a place outdoors where there are plants: "Water moves quickly through potting soil."
- Sample answer to the question of how the material the teacher provided can help soil hold water: "If some of it is mixed with soil it might help."
- Sample observation for comparisons of the soil with and without this material: "The soil still felt moist after 24 hours." Graphs should show reasonable data.

Using Water to Harness Energy

- The energy source for a waterwheel is the moving water, which turns the wheel; that motion makes a mill or other machinery work.
- Materials to model a waterwheel might include craft sticks, fasteners, sticks, and rubber bands. Sketches should reflect a waterwheel that is possible for students to build.
- Sample answer to question of the uses of waterwheels in historical America: "Turning mills that produced cornmeal, ran factories that made cloth, or ground up grain for flour."
- Sample answer to questions of modern uses for energy harnessed from water and future uses for water as an energy source: "Water turns large turbines that produce electrical power for use in businesses and homes."

Freshwater Versus Salt Water

- One of the circles should have an accurate depiction of the Earth, and the other should have a pie chart showing about 75% water versus 25% land on Earth.
- For observations of salt water and freshwater, accept reasonable answers (e.g., invertebrates in both, more floating particles in salt water).
- Accept reasonable answers on the bar graph based on student research.

Animals That Live in Water

- Students may name any animal that lives in water (e.g., fish such as trout or shark; mammal such as a dolphin or whale; reptile such as a turtle).
- Answers to the question of whether all living things can be seen by humans will vary. Some students will say yes; others might say that there are living things that can only be seen by microscopes.
- Answers will vary on the chart comparing the water animal named earlier and a macroinvertebrate observed in this lesson. Students may sketch and use words to describe both.

ANSWER KEY

Measuring Water for a Day

- For the prediction of the amount of water used, accept any reasonable answer (e.g., 25 liters, 10 gallons).
- For the list of activities requiring water, students should put the appropriate number of check marks beside each activity (e.g., three check marks beside "brushing teeth." They should add other activities (e.g., "drinking a glass of water"; "watering Mom's plants").
- Sample answer for comparison of prediction of amount of water used with results (check that answers are three sentences): "I predicted 25 liters but I used 30 liters. It was more. I didn't know that I used so much water brushing teeth."
- Sample answer for two ways to reduce water usage: "(1) I will turn off the water while I am brushing my teeth from now on. (2) I will reduce my shower time."

Droughts

- For the steps being taken to study how a drought affects plants, accept reasonable answers that are ordered and logical. Sample list of steps: (1) We will have two sets of plants: one will get regularly watered, one will not. (2) As much as possible, the plants will start with the same conditions such as type/amount of soil, size of pot, etc. (3) [Continued]
- Students may predict "wilting" or "discoloration" as the first sign of drought. In response to the question of how many days it will be before they notice this sign, accept reasonable answers (e.g., one day, two days).
- Responses to the "What has happened after…?" prompts will depend on the conditions in the experiment your class conducts; sample responses include "no change" and "all leaves wilted."
- Sample answers for comparison of predictions with what happened: "My prediction was correct." The plant started to wilt after two days." "I was wrong. Nothing happened until the fourth day and then it was just slight wilting."

Is There Water in Fruit?

- Students should write down the type of fruit that you provide.
- For predictions of the weight of a fruit, accept reasonable answers (e.g., 30 grams).
- Predictions of what percentage of the fruit's weight is water will vary (e.g., 25%, 50%, 80%).
- For the question on removing water content from fruits or vegetables, if you are drying fruit in a microwave or oven, discuss this with students and let them answer accordingly.
- Weights recorded after the process of removing water will vary depending on the fruit and the process. For example, apple slices might weigh 20 grams after being dried in a microwave.
- Sample answer for the difference in weight and the percentage of the piece of fruit that is water: "The weight went from 30 grams to 20 grams, which is 10 grams difference. So the percentage of the piece of fruit that is water is 10 divided by 30, or 33%."
- Answers to the question of whether the students are surprised at the percentage will vary; accept reasonable answers (e.g., "Yes, I thought it would be more").

ANSWER KEY

Chapter 6: In the Sky

Clouds and Precipitation

- Sample answers for what clouds look like (check for detail): "Puffy white cotton balls fill the sky." "Long grey lines almost look like big feathers."

- Sample answer for prediction of what might happen as a result of these clouds: "The puffy clouds will not result in precipitation but will be blowing away by this time tomorrow."

- Sample answer for comparing a television or internet forecast with students' predictions: "The forecast called for rain but I thought the clouds would move on."

- Sample answer for what actually happened the next day: "It did not rain. The clouds did move on as I had predicted. I didn't think they looked like rain clouds anyway."

- Sample answer to the questions about accuracy of weather forecasts: "No, forecasts can be wrong because they are predicted by humans or computer models. No one can say for certain what will happen, we just make predictions based on evidence."

- Sample answer for what other evidence can be used to predict precipitation: "Temperature—for instance, if the temperature is 10° above freezing, there is almost 100% certainty there will not be snow. If it is below freezing, that is one piece of evidence that supports a prediction of snow."

The Sun and Its Impact on Earth

- For the list of three ways that the Sun helps life on Earth, various answers are acceptable (e.g., makes photosynthesis possible, provides warmth, gives us light to help us see).

- Sample answers for the chart are filled in below:

Container (in order of prediction)	Prediction for Inside Temperature	Actual Temperature After Being in Sunshine
Black can	28°C	30°C
Clear plastic container	27°C	27°C
White envelope	26°C	27°C

- Sample answer for how the results of the experiment were different from what was expected: "The color may have affected the temperature in the can, or it could have been the metal. The temperature in the can was warmer than I thought."

- The following answer, or similar wording, is acceptable for why people are advised to wear dark colors in cold weather or light colors in warm weather: "Dark colors absorb more heat energy than light colors."

ANSWER KEY

How Stars Can Guide Us

- Check that the sketches of the Big Dipper and another constellation are reasonable representations.
- Sample response to the *Follow the Drinking Gourd* prompt: "Since most slaves could not read or write, looking at the stars and finding patterns in the constellations gave them a common 'language' that they could 'read' from anywhere when they were outdoors at night."

Our Solar System

- Check for acceptable answers on the chart; answers will vary depending on the models provided.
- Students need to make two types of motions when modeling movement of planets in the solar system: (a) walking around the Sun is revolving and (b) turning around and around while walking is rotation.
- After doing research on creating a scale model of the solar system, students will likely find that there is no scale model that can fit inside your school building.

Flying Animals

- Sample answers for the chart are filled in below:

Birds	Bats	Flying Insects
Have wings covered in feathers	Have wings covered in skin with some fur	Butterflies have wings covered in scales, dragonflies have nearly clear wings
Birds of prey have keen eyesight	Have heightened sense of hearing and eyes adapted for nighttime	Have compound eyes
Have two legs	Have three legs	Have six legs

- Sample response to the prompt: "If a bat lost the ability to fly, then it would not be able to catch as many insects because it walks more slowly than it flies."

Air Pollution

- For predictions about evidence of pollution, accept any reasonable answer (e.g., "I think dust will stick to the tape and cover most of it." "There will be some pollen, dust, and other unidentified items on the tape catcher.").
- Accept reasonable answers for what will happen after one day, two days, etc. (e.g., "no change" or "a few specks of dust are visible" after one day).
- The sketch should reflect what is listed for the days the pollution catcher was observed.

ANSWER KEY

- Sample description: "At first, there was very little on the tape/pollution catcher. Then after three days it got a lot of dust and maybe some pollen, making it almost completely covered after five days."

How Does Wind Help Us?

- Sample answers for signs of the blowing wind: "Leaves moving in the trees" and "Flag flying on the flagpole."
- Sample answers for why it is important for meteorologists to warn people when they forecast extreme wind conditions: "Because wind is strong and can tear down a house" and "Warning people before severe weather sometimes helps prevent injury."
- The following is an acceptable answer to how the device made by the student is like a windmill: "The wind moves parts of the device just like it moves a windmill."
- Accept reasonable sketches of what happened with the device when using a fan; students should use arrows to show wind movement.

INDEX

INDEX

INDEX

INDEX

NATIONAL SCIENCE TEACHERS ASSOCIATION